ABOUT THE AUTHOR

Mwangala Lethbridge is the Executive Director and Founder of the Mwangala Mwenda Foundation, a Non-Governmental Organisation that was formed with the vision to empower women and children of Kalabo District in rural Zambia.

Mwangala has helped to launch the Dorcas Lundambuyu Lewanika Scholarship, an educational scholarship named to honour her maternal grandmother's legacy, awarded to pupils of high potential from vulnerable households dedicated to expanding their opportunities and creating future leaders in society. A second platform, the Kutwano Empowerment Initiative, provides women with skills training, motivational and mentorship platforms for the youth as well as encouraging adult learning programmes.

Mwangala is a Registered Architect and member of the Zambia Institute of Architects and once served as the vice-president of the Institute. As a private consultant, her career spans over twenty-five years and she uses her expertise in the Foundation to develop projects among vulnerable groups, specifically in relation to addressing rural infrastructure and housing.

A Christian by faith and raised Catholic, her belief system guides her purpose in life which rests on four pillars: taking ownership, reliability, commitment and resilience. She uses these pillars as her cornerstones. Mwangala's leadership aims to inspire change in the lives of those she is blessed to encounter.

Mwangala is a strong advocate for the empowerment of women and youth for personal development opportunities.

Mwangala has earned an MBA from Alliance Manchester Business School, considered as one of the best MBA programmes in the United Kingdom. She also has a Masters in Human Settlements from Katholieke University in Leuven, Belgium.

Mwangala resides both in the United Kingdom with her husband Adam and their three children and in Zambia, where she is pursuing a career in politics.

Connect with Mwangala Lethbridge:

Facebook: Mwangala Lethbridge
Twitter: @mwangalaleth
LinkedIn: www.linkedin.com/in/mwangala-lethbridge-402b5020/
Website: www.mwangalamwendafoundation.org

BOOK REVIEWS

'IT WAS NOT ENOUGH'. Her 'life point' is giving life choices to girls through education. The interviewer said, 'Another Roma Girls Woman Leader!' touched on educating girls in rural western province, Zambia. How being a woman activism was not enough to make a change.

Brilliant memoir – we should try not to minimise anyone's pain or experiences. She explains that 'Trauma is Trauma'. There is no 'big or bigger'. 'Trauma is Trauma.' She touched on overcoming discrimination in the workplace. I laughed at 'we are waiting for the Engineer' and love that she patiently sat and waited, choosing her battles. She says it was not enough to advocate change, she wanted to affect a bigger change, a real impact… through a seat at the table as a Member of Parliament. Showing girls everywhere the value of education and that being a housewife is OK as a CHOICE, and not as the only way out.

Mrs Linda Kalinda

Your courage, strength, humanity and willingness to share your vulnerability makes you an inspiration to us.

We all cried not because we are sad, but because we all relate and celebrate her courage because she is doing what we all want to do but have not done. Her strength gives us strength. Her courage encourages us not to give up. If she is it, we will do it. One step at a time. One day at a time. And she is still standing. Look at her now – in spite of her brokenness she still stands and challenges the scars of brokenness, Mwangala Mwenda Lethbridge is unbroken, she has defied her physical challenges because true champions are knocked down but never knocked out because their strength is in their spirit and championship mentality.

Mwangala is a champion. Our champion. Champion of the girl child, champion of those life has broken champion against the odds. She shines and we cry for joy victory over death and her defiance and refusal to stay down.

You are still standing. I celebrate you. God bless you.

Pastor Jolomi

This isn't just a memoir, or a self-help book, it is a generous gift to the reader. I have the privilege of knowing Mwangala and the honour of being her niece. Reading this book, I felt many of the same emotions I felt on 28th April 2019, following behind her and Notulu for a few miles of the London Marathon: awe, wonder, pride, inspiration, and the knowledge that truly anything is possible if you are determined and allow others to help you. In her writing as in life, Mwangala demonstrates the power of vulnerability and the bravery of honest self-reflection. There are many lessons shared in *Still Standing*, but if you just hear one let it be that there is always another chapter of your story and you hold the pen with which to write it.

Lucy Scanlon

A very honest account which makes one stop to think and assess one's life.

I am filled with admiration for Mwangala Mwenda Lethbridge and I hope she now cries less.

Clara Mvula

STILL STANDING

THE FLIP SIDE OF DENIAL, DEPRESSION AND FORGIVENESS

MWANGALA MWENDA LETHBRIDGE

Copyright © 2022 Mwangala Mwenda Lethbridge

The moral right of the author has been asserted.

Apart from any fair dealing for the purposes of research or private study, or criticism or review, as permitted under the Copyright, Designs and Patents Act 1988, this publication may only be reproduced, stored or transmitted, in any form or by any means, with the prior permission in writing of the publishers, or in the case of reprographic reproduction in accordance with the terms of licences issued by the Copyright Licensing Agency. Enquiries concerning reproduction outside those terms should be sent to the publishers.

Matador
Unit E2 Airfield Business Park,
Harrison Road, Market Harborough,
Leicestershire. LE16 7UL
Tel: 0116 2792299
Email: books@troubador.co.uk
Web: www.troubador.co.uk/matador
Twitter: @matadorbooks

ISBN 978 1803130 033

British Library Cataloguing in Publication Data.
A catalogue record for this book is available from the British Library.

Printed and bound by CPI Group (UK) Ltd, Croydon, CR0 4YY
Typeset in 12pt Minion Pro by Troubador Publishing Ltd, Leicester, UK

Matador is an imprint of Troubador Publishing Ltd

To my sisters, Linda, Lungowe, Notulu, and Priscilla,
who dropped their worlds to hold up mine.

Disclaimer

The events and incidents in this book are a true reflection of my recollection relating to my accident. The people mentioned herein have given their express consent and approval to be included in this narrative. Any events that may not match other people's recollection are purely coincidental and only reflect my perception of them. They are in no way meant to undermine or denigrate anyone who played a part in my recovery.

TABLE OF CONTENTS

FOREWORD — XI
PROLOGUE — XIII

PART ONE – DENIAL

1	THIRD DECEMBER	3
2	SACRIFICE	13
3	MOUNTAIN PRAISE	23
4	CULTURAL DILEMMA	29
5	MOUNT KILIMANJARO	35

PART TWO – DEPRESSION

6	#JUSTLIVE	43
7	ROCK BOTTOM	47
8	SHAME	55
9	FIRST TIME SINCE	59
10	MY HEART WILL HEAL	65
11	NOTHING IS EASY	71
12	TEAM BEACH	75

13	ONE DAY AT A TIME	83
14	I AM NOT A DUCK	93
15	CAMPFIRE	95
16	NINA	101
17	CHRISTOPHER	107
18	AJ	111
19	TRANSFORMER	115
20	SHAKEN	119

PART THREE – FORGIVENESS

21	WHAT NEXT?	129
22	NOT FULLY GROWN	133
23	A PIECE OF JEWELLERY	139
24	IT'S THERE IF YOU ASK	143
25	PREGABALIN VS MBA	147
26	NOT WELCOME HERE	151
27	GETTING BETTER	155
28	AUTHENTIC	159
29	NUMBERS	163
30	THE SMALL PRINT	165
31	SADNESS	171
32	TEN SECONDS	175
33	PHYSIO, PHYSIO, AND SO MUCH MORE PHYSIO	181
34	HOW TO LOSE AN ELECTION	185
35	LONDON MARATHON	191
36	BLESSED ASSURANCE	197

| ACKNOWLEDGEMENTS | 201 |
| BIBLIOGRAPHY | 203 |

FOREWORD

Mwangala is a strong woman and full of fire. In my interaction with her she impresses me as a person who can be relentless in chasing her dreams be it in her professional career as an Architect and in politics in particular. She has not been deterred by all the trials she has endured.

When I visited Mwangala in hospital following the road traffic accident where the motorcycle she was riding collided with a speeding motor vehicle, I expected to find her in a state of helplessness as her injuries were beyond imagination. When I approached her bed, she recognized me and greeted me with a smile though in great pain. It was unbelievable that someone who the day before was on the verge of death with broken limbs would master a smile, I could only conclude that this young woman was was a true warrior with a strong will power, a courageous and undefeatable human being with a fighting spirit.

I am aware also that she has been disappointed and hurt by the political system she trusted. Mwangala, please don't let the pain of an imperfect past hinder the glory of your future. You are so much more powerful than you may currently understand.

Mrs. Inonge Mutukwa Wina
Former Vice President of the Republic of Zambia

PROLOGUE

The election results began to pour in at about 7pm that evening after the last ballot was cast. I could hear my mother praying in the other room as I watched my father with his ear pressed to the two-band radio and shouting out each count as it came in. It slowly dawned on me that the result would not be in my favour. Polling station after polling station announced their results and I began to pack my clothes in readiness for the trip back to the main district. The rest of the team was outside by the fire sitting in silence; then there was a gentle knock on my door, and I heard the words, 'Honourable, we need to go now.'

I rolled my eyes, grateful for the darkness as I had asked them on countless occasions not to call me by that title, to no avail.

'But it's 2am!' I protested.

'Yes, but we have to leave now before they come.'

I was tempted to ask who 'they' were, but I knew better. I picked up my bag, and gently shook my mother's shoulder, who had at this point fallen asleep, and whispered, 'Mum, Dad, we have to leave.'

We left quietly and the only sound heard was that of the Land Rover crossing the sandy plains towards the pontoon on the Luanginga river. We had ensured that the pontoon operators would be on our side of the river to cross quickly for the victory lap after our anticipated win, but alas, it was for the great escape. I thanked my team, turned to my family said my goodbyes and watched them hold back their tears as I did mine.

'It's okay, Mummy, don't cry,' I whispered, hugging her tightly and not wanting to let go, as the waves of the Luanginga river splashed against the sides of the pontoon, rocking us gently.

It was now 4am, and I remembered I had not called my husband to tell him the election results. It would be 3am in the UK, but I knew he would not be sleeping, so I called and instantly heard my son's sleepy voice.

'Hello Mummy, it's Christopher. Did you win?'

'I didn't, but that's okay, we ran a good race. Please, tell Daddy I called.'

The anxiety of the elections really began my journey of self-discovery, which was also a wake-up call of what was going on around me.

This memoir is a journey of self-discovery. It is an acknowledgement that we are never isolated in the experiences we have as we journey back and forth in time and battle between our old and new selves.

This process of self-discovery is my journey, to show how I fought my fight after destroyed opportunities and reinvented myself to learn how to hold on. I had been bruised so heavily from holding on so tightly that I needed to have a conversation between my old self and my new self.

This is a reflection where there is no one to blame.

It is the flip side of my denial, depression, and forgiveness, and finding my purpose.

PART ONE
DENIAL

'The thing about denial is that it doesn't feel like denial when it's going on.'

Georgina Kleege

CHAPTER ONE

THIRD DECEMBER

'I have come to accept the feeling of not knowing where I am going. And I have trained myself to love it. Because it is only when we are suspended in mid-air with no landing in sight, that we force our wings to unravel and alas begin our flight. And as we fly, we still may not know where we are going to. But the miracle is in the unfolding of the wings. You may not know where you're going, but you know that, so long as you spread your wings, the winds will carry you.'

C. JoyBell C.

My eyes open slowly to the soundtrack of singing birds going about their morning rituals and the chirping of crickets in the distance; I lazily stretch across my bed and begin to smile in anticipation of this morning's ride. My husband calls it my midlife crisis, but after a blissful six hours of sleep, I prefer to call it the joy of being alive and the promise of God's Grace.

It is 4am; this is my favourite part of the day as I am able to enjoy the small things that pass me by because of the usual bustle of everyday life. I am already on my third cup of tea. My thoughts quickly go to the meeting I will have later in the day, and so I lay out my outfit in advance – a process that always takes me forever only to end up with the same pair of jeans and my favourite shirt. I can already hear Adam's voice in my head complaining about why I buy so many clothes and still end up wearing one of his shirts. With the appropriate answer still eluding me, I head off towards Ian's house where I left my bike from the last time we went riding. It is now 5am and I find Ian already dressed for the ride, and both bikes are already warming up, rumbling smoothly.

'Would you like a cup of tea before we head out?' he asks with a wide grin knowing full well that I would never say no to a cup of tea.

'No thanks, I've already had my fair share for now. I just need to change quickly,' I say as my eyes dart around to find a spot where I can have some privacy, but we look at each other and Ian lets out a hearty laugh.

'It's okay, you can go inside, there's no one there.'

We both understand why he had to add the disclaimer and we smile it off. As I get ready, we chuckle about how the other riders always think I overdress for the ride. They believe, sooner rather than later, my bike will not be able to carry my weight with the additional kilos due to all the protective clothing I wear on our bike rides.

'Okay, I'm ready…' I happily step outside, but it almost slipped my mind, 'wait,' I shout, 'one last thing, my back protector,' and we both smile as I hand him the keys to my car that I have parked in his yard. It is a safety measure we follow in case I fall during one of our rides. The irony of that routine was to prove so surreal.

All geared up, the car locked, and the bike perfectly warmed and ready, we leave Chalala, a newly zoned residential area boasting all types of custom-built houses. We continue past Woodlands, another beautiful residential area. Woodlands: the tar roads here are beautifully lined with mature 'Flame' and 'Jacaranda' trees that burst with blossom of little clusters of purple and red flowers in September. On this December morning as we approach the New Kasama Road, it is a beautiful sunny morning and there is barely any traffic, which gives us the pleasure of having an uninterrupted ride. How delightful, especially compared to when the roads are, more often than not, choked with constant streams of cars, buses, trucks, and funeral processions, which we never go past as a last sign of respect to the unknown loved person. We pass the usual police checkpoints after the American School, and soon we are on the new road heading toward Chiawa, Lusaka Rural. I cherish our early morning rides in the countryside, when the world and all its roadside goats are still asleep. With such a clear road, you can take in the beauty and magnificence of the landscape and the crisp, fresh morning breeze that is felt even in my biker's gear. I open my visor, lifting my face towards the sky, to feel the morning sunbeams on my face for a fleeting moment. I smile. I let out a deep exhale as I utter the words, 'Thank you, Jesus.'

Earlier on, I had asked Ian to carry his partner Barbara along on the ride because I knew it would slow him down, and with someone on his pillion seat, I am taking the lead this time. It is a position I have secretly coveted for a while and finally have been granted. Thank goodness for partners. We often joked about how he was my guardian angel with the way he insisted on taking the lead position during the rides, since he was a more experienced rider. I am a better rider than he actually believes, but the idea of having someone to alert me to the lone goat or cow that thinks the grass is greener on the other side just as you approach, is definitely worth letting him think I am not that good a rider.

I love this particular route we have taken because of its scenic rolling hills, which appear blue in the distance, and the morning mist seems to float as it is burned away by the warmth of the rising sun. The rich, earthy scent of the newly cultivated farmland rises to my nostrils, a smell that reminds me that I am home – the country of my birth – as the long arms of waving green leaves stretching from the maize stalks sway in the morning breeze as though waving at us. The serenity and the silence are a marvel that is interrupted only by the deep howl of our motorbikes.

On my Honda CBR 600, it is a clear route to accelerate from zero to eighty in less than three seconds, and the bike can equally as easily stop for that one stubborn animal that decides to wake up before the others to look for a blade of grass across the road. I smile behind my helmet as I watch Ian doing a 'wheelie' past me even with his girlfriend, Barbara, on the back; he cannot help himself. I am laughing because my pole position has not lasted as long as I hoped; but I enjoyed it, however short-lived.

I slow down and pull over to the side to make a quick phone call and Ian goes past me, busy showing off – doing his thing – with Barbara holding on for dear life. I take off my helmet and make the call. It rings twice but there is silence on the other end, and it goes straight to voicemail. Perhaps it is too early for a Saturday morning call, and I am certain that everyone is having a lie-in. I put my helmet back on and remember to switch off my phone. 'No distraction as we ride' has always been our rule. When you are on two wheels, every sense is engaged one hundred per cent, and on a motorbike, one does not have the luxury of becoming absent-minded as might be the case on a long car drive; those few stolen seconds when we can drift off to make plans or go over something that creeps on our minds. Today, I am on a bike, and my senses are fully heightened. A few moments later, I catch up with Ian, who has pulled over to the side for a 'pit-stop'. As I slow down, he gives me the thumbs up, so I nod in acknowledgment and accelerate smoothly past him, revelling in the power and control of the machine beneath me.

I know for a fact that it will only take a few seconds before he blasts past me like a bat, taunting me, but my brother Nyambe's words echo in my ear: 'Respect your bike and it will respect you.' And on more than one occasion he would say to me: 'Always ride your own ride, Mwangala,' and today, on this glory-filled morning, I do just that. I ride my own ride joyfully, deliberately, taking in the beautiful view of the countryside and relishing the morning breeze. I reflect on how good it is to be back home and when I have smiled enough, squeeze the accelerator handle to increase my speed and instinctively hunch over to minimise the wind shear.

A quick glance through my rear-view mirror and Ian is still not within sight, so I sit up to look around – sprawling hills, winding roads, rocky cliffs, and the smell of burning charcoal filling my helmet causing me to open the visor so I can catch a breath of fresh air. I begin the descent down a long gradual hill when I see an oncoming vehicle in the distance; I think nothing of it. As it draws closer, I push my visor down and prepare for the on-pass, but the vehicle begins to turn into my lane.

Lord, why is he turning? Where is he going? What is he doing? All these racing thoughts and questions to the universe go through my mind as the oncoming vehicle is now clearly in front of me. A sudden coldness grips my whole body despite the warm sun rising and every muscle in my body screams at me to jump off my bike, but I remain frozen in the moment, knowing there is nowhere to go. I do not panic even as I see it turn towards me and as life slowly turns to slow motion, I fall into an altered state of consciousness. My spirit leaves my body and I see with clarity my impending demise that lies before me and I become paralysed by fear. I close my eyes to dissociate myself from this reality, for there is no amount of training or experience that could have prepared me or prevented what was about to happen.

There it was. The huge, thunderous sound of screeching tyres mixed with the ear-splitting scream of a woman in the distance. I hear it, I do not feel it, but I hear it. The sound of colliding metallic contact with something I cannot identify. Again, I hear it, I do not feel it! I wonder what the deafening noise is because it is unbelievably, impossibly, loud. It is so loud that I can hear the crushing noise of breaking parts, but my mind still cannot relate or register it and the tornado sweeps me up into its twisted violent embrace and I am caught up in it – I am in a tornado, turning and twisting and failing to control my arms, my legs, and I'm left in a confused state, feeling like a rag doll.

Lord, why can't I control my arms? Lord, there are no tornados in Zambia. Lord, what is happening? But there is absolute silence – total and absolute silence and as if the universe has whispered something to the warm African skies, the violent winds have stopped, and I am no longer a rag doll. There I was, floating peacefully in a relaxed almost Zen-like moment of stillness that seemed to stretch on forever. The deep silence of the air caresses my body; I am floating in a peaceful but deadly bubble.

The woman's horrifying screams in the distance manage to pierce the bubble of solitude I am engulfed in, but I do not know why she is screaming. *Lord, why is Barbara screaming? Why is she making so much noise? Why has she disturbed my sleep?* and the only reply to my questions were more screams.

Wake up, Mwangala. Very slowly, I open my eyes and find myself in mid-air and immediately panic.

The realisation of my state breaks my safety net and I begin to fall. Once more I am caught up in the tornado and my arms are swinging wildly and I begin to lose control of my twisting torso, but in that confused state I am granted one last moment of clarity and I pray a single line: *Lord, do not take me, my children still need me*, and almost immediately I hit the ground with a thud… BOOM!… with such force that it tears the wind out of me. The crushing sound is now twice amplified, and my ears are ringing. The taste of blood fills my mouth as I roll downwards, uncontrollably, and finally I hit into something that breaks my fall with an even louder sound than before… BOOOOOOOM!

I am caught between two levels of consciousness, but I cannot move, so I just lay lie there nothing doing. I try to focus myself on being present, but I dare not open my eyes. So, I continue the conversation with the only person Who is with me now and ask: *Lord, if I open my eyes, what will I see?* but He does not answer. Though alone, I feel His presence with me. I am certain of this, but then, why doesn't He answer me? Slowly, I gain the courage to open my eyes and I see what appears to be my right arm dangling above my head in a twisted and seemingly impossible position. I'm wondering if it is still attached to my body, so I continue with my mindless conversation: *Okay Lord, if I can move my fingers, then that arm is still attached to me.* I hesitate before I try… and mercifully, my fingers move and a wave of relief passes through me, so I dare to look beyond my helmet to the rest of my body.

I see a breathtakingly beautiful bed of little red wildflowers flowing from an opening in my boot and become mesmerised by the river as it continues to pour its magical petals, '*Oh, what pretty red flowers flowing from my boot, but why are they there?*' Again, silence. After what seems like an eternity, it dawns on me that they are not red petals, but it is my blood gushing out from an opening in my boot and my heart begins to race. Suddenly, I am gasping for air and I begin to panic because I'm left wondering why my helmet is choking me. It is getting tighter.

Lord, I can't breathe, and I cry out again, *Lord, help me. I can't breathe*, as a tear rolls down my cheek.

Mwangala, open your eyes.

I look up and come face to face with a stranger who is trying to pull the helmet off my head, and I let out what I think is a scream, but no sound is made. All the pain suddenly hits me. I can feel it now, that sound I had heard earlier – that thunderous, crushing sound – it was the sound of my body breaking. I scream, and again, no sound comes out. Instinctively, I want to panic but I realise it may be the last soundless scream I make. Instead, I let out a desperate whisper: '*Munipaya.*' I know the stranger is trying to help me, but it feels like he is trying to kill me, and then I hear a man's voice shout, '*Ali moyo! Ni mu kadzi!*' confirming I'm still alive and I'm a woman. I have no idea what the relevance is at this stage that I am woman, but somehow, the revelation of a woman in a biker's suit crashing on a motorbike increases the clamour tenfold.

Everyone is shouting in unanimity, '*Ni mu kadzi!*' repeatedly.

'*Pa* Honda?' another asks, questioning whether I was on a motorbike as though confirmation might elicit a different response.

'*Imwe, sanga peme. Chosani chisote,*' another suggests, realising that the helmet with the visor down must be blocking my air flow and preventing me from breathing. The first man begins pulling the helmet off my head again, and I begin to shake uncontrollably as I begin to choke. Then I realise if I do not stop screaming, he will either kill or paralyse me, but I chastise myself: *Stop screaming, Mwangala, and think. You survived the fall, now move your hand*, and then I move my left hand. *Oh Lord, it can move*, and I lift the visor.

'Where is Ian?' I enquire helplessly, now looking at the other faces in my view.

The man pulling the helmet shouts at the top of his voice, '*Ali moyo! Afuna bazanke!*' He has the intuition to know what I want, and he lets go of the helmet and runs off looking for my friends. Now I can breathe properly. The crowd parts and then I see Ian. The worry, fear, pain, and anguish on his face are terribly clear to see. He makes me see everything I am afraid of, and I am thinking, 'I must be badly broken,' then I hear him whisper.

'*Bo* Mwangala, what should I do?'

'Call an ambulance.'

'*Bo* Mwangala, who should I call?'

'Ian, call my brother.'

'Where is he?'

'He's in Zanzibar!'

Ian comes closer to my face in an attempt to make me realise that calling Zanzibar at this point will not make much sense, but I am panicking and instead I plead, 'Ian, don't let me bleed to death; please don't leave me; please don't take off my helmet; please don't touch me; Ian, it hurts everywhere.'

I can feel my brokenness, then suddenly, all that fear I saw earlier leaves his face and he disappears from my sight. It feels like a lifetime, but a few moments later, Ian returns to my side.

'*Bo* Mwangala, there's no ambulance, but there is an Officer going to Mikango Barracks who has volunteered to let us take the taxi he was using so that we can go to the hospital.'

'No Ian, call an ambulance.'

'*Bo* Mwangala, we don't have much time,' he insists.

'Ian don't let me die,' I plead.

He requests the men now standing around us to carry me towards the waiting taxi, and the first person to touch my arm drops it in fright when

I scream loudly from the excruciating pain that rips through my body, except this time, I can hear the deafening sound of my own scream. Ian comes closer to me.

'I'm sorry, be strong,' he says, and instructs the other men. 'One – two – three – lift!' I hear him shout.

There are arms everywhere, and in one swoop, I am lifted out of the drain that broke my fall, and we are heading towards the waiting vehicle. I cannot stop screaming when I realise again that the deafening sound is coming from me.

The pain is intense and overwhelming, and I pray for the sweet loss of consciousness. They are pushing from one door and pulling from the other trying to lay me across the back seat of the saloon car. Still, I do not pass out.

Barbara is still screaming, and Ian says to her firmly, 'Sit in the front and go with her. I'm coming behind you.'

We are speeding off in the Eastern direction towards the hospital, and I can feel the car swerving from left to right. The manic driver must be purposely overtaking cars in the traffic, which is getting busier. I ask Barbara to gently pull the phone, which miraculously has not cracked from the impact, out of my inner pocket and phone Dr Usha.

'What's her number?'

'It's in the phone,' I whisper through the searing pain.

There is a moment of silence, then I hear Barbara's voice…

'Hello? Hello? Is that Dr Usha?' (Silence)

'This is *Bo* Mwangala's phone. She has been involved in an accident and we are on our way to CFB.' (Silence)

She begins to cry and she is whispering, 'Doctor, she's bad,' but not low enough because I can hear her, and I am relieved that, at last, I am drifting away. My eyes start to close slowly and I can feel the peace that comes with it. I am longing so much to sleep, but somehow, I am aware of what that sleep will mean so I start whispering desperately to myself in between breaths, '*Wake up, Mwangala! Nina still needs you. Wake up, Mwangala! Christopher still needs you. Wake up, Mwangala! AJ still needs you.* Barbie?'

'Yes, *Bo* Mwangala.'

'Please call my husband.'

As my eyes close, tears begin to flow silently within my helmet.

'Heaven did not seem to be my home; and I broke my heart with weeping to come back to earth; and the angels were so angry that they flung me out into the middle of the heath on the top of Wuthering Heights; where I woke sobbing for joy.'

Emily Brontë'

CHAPTER TWO
SACRIFICE

'Hope in reality is the worst of all evils because it prolongs the torments of man.'

Friedrich Nietzsche[2]

The iconic Leopard's Hill Road that passes through the affluent residential area of New Kasama winds through beautiful undulating hills towards the Lower Zambezi Valley, an area that gives rise to one of Zambia's distinctive traits – the Lower Zambezi National Park[3] – with elephant herds, sometimes up to one hundred strong, hippo, leopard, lion, buffalo and over 400 bird species that all gather in a mesmerising wilderness. It offers a stark but welcome contrast to the chaos of the congested urban roads of Lusaka. The Pave Zambia 2000 project, which by all accounts is a great stretch of well-constructed tarmac, is helping to decongest the inner-city roads, most of which are in various stages of disrepair, with the majority of Lusaka's roads having neither storm water drains nor culverts. How ironic, therefore, that my ride on that Saturday morning would end up in a storm water drain along that very length of new road network.

I have come to understand during my recovery that the 'tornado', which lifted me high into that invisible funnel and threw me dozens of metres away and finally crash-landed me inside the cold concrete drain, was the tremendous impact of the car against the entire right side of my body, and somewhere in between was my motorbike.

I am drifting in and out of consciousness, and the journey feels agonisingly long, as it seems as if we will never reach our destination. I am screaming and praying, then more screaming, and even more desperate praying. The unknown taxi driver remains silent throughout the trip, concentrating fiercely like a rally driver as he weaves away from the serene landscape of New Kasama towards the chaos of Bauleni high-density area. It is an area where mini-buses stop anywhere including the middle of the road – hooting and honking to get the attention of the lone pedestrian who might be their next passenger. I can hear them from the back seat of the car where I lie bleeding, as they shout out 'Town, town, town! *Mu yenda?*' The disregard for traffic rules is regrettably common in these parts, playing cat and mouse with traffic officers, and I guess this morning is no exception. I can feel the taxi go off the tarmac onto the gravel bypass, the driver's hand on the horn, pedestrians scampering and hurling insults at him not knowing the reason for his manic driving that I am secretly grateful for.

He must seem an unruly driver, a perception associated with most mini-bus and taxi drivers in Zambia. He slows down briefly, trying to find a way to get past a funeral procession at the Leopard's Hill Cemetery, and soon cuts a path on the side road only to encounter a traffic jam at the intersection of Crossroads Shopping Mall four-way road. Undeterred by the traffic emerging from the minor road, he somehow manoeuvres the car safely past the chaos and on to the clearer major road towards Longacres area and the clinic.

After what seems like an eternity, we arrive at the clinic, horn still blaring; the waiting doctors and nurses are already in the car park having been alerted earlier on by Barbara's call to Dr Usha, who is now also waiting for my arrival The taxi doors fly open and I hear a gasp and can feel someone begin to pull my legs in an attempt to get me out of the car, but I scream so loudly from the pain that the person drops my legs and blood continues to gushes out from the torn boot. Where is that loss of consciousness that I have seen so many times in movies? Why can I not drift into a blissful sleep and wake up in a clean hospital bed and ask, 'What happened?', but all that is in vain – at least for me. I am fully conscious; I feel every touch and movement of the nurses who are now trying to remove me from the car as carefully as they possibly can. They take a hold of my arm, the arm that I am no longer certain is still attached to the rest of my body, and I let out an even more piercing scream. The sight of my body covered in blood causes a sea of anxiety within me and I am hoping that it is not my blood. Suddenly, my sister Noti's face appears above mine, caressing my face through the opening of the visor whilst her lips are moving, saying something I cannot hear.

'Noti, please show them how to take my boots off,' I tell my sister in a whisper. 'Noti, please take off my helmet because I cannot breathe. Noti, please take me out of this car, am feeling cold,' I plead desperately, feeling drained as the taste of bile in my mouth begins to rise.

Her face disappears as quickly as it appeared and I call out in a panic; 'Noti, don't go, please don't leave me,' and then I hear them count out loudly, 'One – two – three' in what now seems like a lifting routine that guides the process, and a lightning bolt of pain pierces right through my body.

Finally, I am out of the car and being pushed by several nurses through to the double doors of the emergency room that burst open as I hear another counting routine that is followed by the now all too familiar: 'One – two – three'. I hold my breath in anticipation of the horrifying lightning bolt of pain.

'My arm! My legs! My back! Please don't touch me!' I cry out loudly, not sure which hurts more than the other. Any part of my body that is touched even slightly sends a bolt of pain right through my body. I begin to shake involuntarily, and the doctor quickly asks the nurse to cut my trousers so they can examine the extent of my injuries. Then I see Usha again. I reach out toward her with the arm that can move and begin to pull and claw at her face. She holds my arm down and firmly places it onto the bed and says something to the others that I cannot comprehend. She starts to walk away.

'Usha, don't leave me; don't let me die,' I say to her, pleadingly with my arm stretched out towards her again.

She looks straight at me and says firmly, 'You will not die,' and walks out. I am now feeling helpless and utterly drained, seemingly alone with my agony and no longer crying but producing a prolonged moan and through the chaotic scene, I see a familiar face. It is Dr Shapi, whom I have visited on previous routine checks, but this flurry of examinations I am undergoing is different and confusing.

'Dr Shapi,' I whisper, 'please, don't let me die. My children…' but she interrupts me mid-sentence and she says in a controlled calm voice: 'Mwangala, try to stay calm. I need you to breathe. Your heart rate needs to come down. You are losing blood and all I need from you now is to focus on your breathing.' She says this repeatedly, each time calmly and gently through the entire process. So much is going on and I keep seeing different faces and hearing different voices, but I try to focus on the one heavenly voice that keeps reassuring and reminding me to breathe. With all the chaos around me, Dr Shapi's tone never changed once. It was her usual gentle, soft spoken voice in my ear, repeatedly whispering, 'Just breathe, Mwangala, just breathe.'

'*Ashu, mawe nashwa. Ima nashwa. Ashu maweeey boma,*' I cry out for my mother, who I need the most now. I can barely shout anymore, and I feel my strength draining, and then suddenly, the pain is gone. I can see clearly and just as clearly, I can hear the different voices of the medical staff surrounding me, but I fail to utter a word. I do not know what is happening to me, but I am conscious. The serenity I felt at that moment was perhaps the eerie feeling of the calm before the storm.

The doctor asks one of the nurses, 'What's that banging at the door?'

'It's her mother, doctor,' she says. 'She's going crazy out there. She's trying to come inside.'

'Do not open that door, no matter what,' the doctor says. It is more of a command than a request.

The doctor is perfectly aware that if my elderly mother sees me in my current state, he will probably have two patients to treat. The agony I am in would immediately be shared by her, and her anguish would kill her; that much I know. Her fierce love for her daughter would be uncontrolled and no restraint in the clinic would keep her from holding me in her arms, and I was just as desperate to be comforted by her, but all I feel is the cold embrace of death that I am fighting against.

Mummy, can you hear me? Did you hear me scream out for you? Mummy, I cannot move. Am I dying? I am crying out, but no one can hear me because my screams are locked inside me. What I am hearing are my own screaming thoughts and pleas, but it is her I am hoping will hear my scream. She knows me and knows how much I need her right now.

The doctor walks out to my waiting family and declares bluntly, 'She's injured here, fractured here, crushed here and broken here,' as he points to most of the areas of his body for illustration. My family are scared and confused. Notulu, whom I fondly call Noti for short, gathers some courage and asks the doctor what he means by 'broken' and 'fractured'.

He shrugs and simply says, 'What does it matter? She's broken everywhere,' and hurries off to call the surgeon, leaving my mother who has collapsed to the floor wailing '*Mawee mwanake washwaaa*' to all who can hear – and all who can't. I see my sisters Noti and Lungowe trying to calm her down as they wheel me towards the operating theatre to try to close the main wounds and control the bleeding. Then suddenly, a random voice is shouting out.

'Stop! Professor Mulla said he will see her straight away. I have brought an ambulance to take her to the Italian Hospital, and they are waiting for her there.'

I turn my head slowly toward the voice and it is Steve. Steve was initially my brother's friend, who over the years took his position as a family member. I can tell he is trying hard not to look directly at me as he has noticed that I am now staring directly at him. I want to call out to him but again, no sound emerges. My mouth is completely dry, and now Flex, a friend, is saying something but I cannot hear him. The surgeon quickly updates the paramedics on my condition, and they prepare to transport me to the specialist hospital in Longacres just a few kilometres away. It is common knowledge that Professor Mulla is recognised as an excellent orthopaedic surgeon in the country, and looking at my current state, and his long waiting list, I am fortunate enough that he is willing to attend to me.

The ambulance ride to the orthopaedic hospital is mercifully uneventful, but I feel a blessed wave of relief when my mother is finally allowed to be by my side as she travels with me. She never once lets go of my hand, her eyes tightly closed keeping back the tears. I watch her as her lips move slowly in silent prayer. All I hear is an occasional, 'Jesus, have mercy,' with a forceful exhalation through her pursed lips. I know the hopelessness that my aged mother feels right now. 'My poor mummy, you want me to live for you, just as much as I want to live for my children.' I am overwhelmed by emotion and begin to wonder, *When do you stop being your parents' child?* And in that moment, crying and trying to soothe my mother incoherently, I knew that you never do. '*Ashu maweee, bo ma,*' slowly and repeatedly, is all I manage to let out.

Finally, we arrive, and Professor Mulla takes an apparently casual glance at me as the paramedics wheel me towards a side ward and instructs the nurse to check my haemoglobin level. One part of me is relieved to be in 'good hands' and another, a much larger part, is utterly terrified of going under. A few moments pass, and the nurses come and go as they collect samples from one arm and insert cannulas on the other. I wait to be taken to the operating theatre, but no one comes bursting through the double doors my eyes are firmly glued on.

'Noti, why am I still lying here? Noti, why aren't they taking me to the operating theatre?' I ask her in a veiled whisper.

Mum is standing in a corner with Priscilla; they are looking at me, looking as scared as I am feeling. I cannot tell what they're thinking, feeling or seeing. Then it dawns on me that my situation must be grave. Their silence tells me as much. It is impossible for my family to remain silent in a situation such as this (or in any situation), yet here they are, just numbly staring at me. No one utters a word.

'Noti, why am I not going to the operating room? *Kin'gi hape*,' I repeat my earlier question.

'*Bo* Mwangala, your Hb level is 3. Professor Mulla has refused to operate on you until you get a blood transfusion,' she says with utter helplessness in her voice.

'Then why aren't they giving me blood, Noti?' In my hazy crazy mind, it is not making any sense – why am I lying here instead of being taken to the operating room?

Her eyes are filled with tears and she whispers, '*Bo* Mwangala, there is no blood at the blood bank, but *Bo* Richard has gone to take another look,' and this time, she cannot contain her emotions. The tears slowly roll down her cheeks as she looks at me helplessly and slowly buries her head into the side of my bed squeezing my free hand. I hear some muffled crying and turn to see my mother and Priscilla with both their heads buried in their hands.

Priscilla, the prayer warrior of the family. The one sister you call on at any family function or fundraiser to be the one to pray when no one offers themselves. Always ready, always faithful, always reminding us about the Grace of God.

Priscilla, my adopted sister, why are you crying?

Notulu makes the decision to make an appeal on Facebook and asks anyone and everyone if they could help by donating blood for her sister who has been in an accident and is in desperate need of O-positive blood. How ironic, given that, prior to my accident, I was never one to be on social media of any kind. My lack of technological skills had always been the excuse for what my family called my antisocial behaviour – an opinion I did not agree with as I simply preferred to spend my time watching 'McDreamy'[4]. So, Notulu makes the appeal on Facebook deciding it would be best to deal with my backlash at a more appropriate time. She just needed me to stay alive, a life-saving decision. 'Sticks and stones will break your bones, but words will never hurt you' – words that have been a comfort to generations of children, and from which she must have drawn her strength, for sure.

The Facebook appeal went out and people responded immediately and in droves. The technician at the blood bank called in his friend who was on leave at the time and asked for the extra set of hands; not only was the line too long to handle alone, but it was also an emergency for the recipient. The compassion and the selfless acts of kindness shown to me, a random stranger to some and Notulu's sister to others, still stirs a powerful emotion within me to this day.

Hours go by and still the surgery does not happen even after what I think is pint after pint of blood has been transfused into me. Surely, it should be enough by now, but it continues throughout the night as the nurses replace each empty bag with a full one. I am so tired from watching the different nurses practising the same routine. Walk in, look at me, look at bag, squeeze bag, turn off something along the length of the tube connecting the bag to my arm, replace bag, turn it back on, tap my wrist. Different nurse, press repeat. Lord I am so tired and each time I close my eyes to rest, Notulu, who is holding my hand, tugs at me gently and begins to narrate some random seemingly irrelevant childhood stories.

'*Bo* Mwangala, do you remember that time when Dad bought us ice cream?' she asks, trying to keep me awake and not lose consciousness as instructed by the medical personnel.

'Noti, I'm tired.'

'Yes, I know you're tired, but do you remember when Nyambe stole Dad's car keys?'

'Noti, please, I just want to sleep,' and I begin what I think is crying, but it is this inaudible moan, and Noti says, 'Okay, *Bo* Mwangala, I've stopped, but I just want you to remember when Dad brought Romeo and Juliet home,' and thus went the whole night till 5am.

Professor Mulla's decision, immediate and firm, almost certainly saved my life although at the time it caused the family great distress. He walks into the room and I hear him mumbling something to the nurses behind the curtain and he lets out an alarmingly loud, 'She's alive? Quick get her to the operating room.'

Wait. What? What do you mean by 'She's alive'? Of course, I'm alive.

My Hb level is now 8 and Professor Mulla says, 'It's not great, but we have to close those wounds to prevent infection.'

I undergo the first of many operations to come. I am given an epidural to ensure I am fully conscious throughout the surgery; there were concerns owing to my extremely low blood count. One doctor is monitoring closely, standing by my head and talking to me, but I can hear the conversation going on in the theatre room.

'Bring me the pin.'

I hear shuffling of the feet. The nurse brings the pin.

'Not this one; I need a bigger one.'

'Professor we don't have a bigger size.'

'Just bring that one, it's okay.'

My half-sedated self is thinking how on earth that could be okay. 'It's the wrong one,' I want to scream out, but I assume the respectful position of silence in such instances.

What is the point anyway? I have no strength to cry any more. I am still producing a constant sort of moan and groan, a horrible combination of weakness and pain, and through all this, everyone including the doctor insists on constantly telling me inane stories.

Meanwhile, my husband is in the UK, frantic on the phone trying to get me evacuated to the UK, but Professor Mulla is reluctant to discharge me before I am stabilised. He compromises and says they can only airlift me to Johannesburg, which is only a four-hour trip in the air ambulance, but I am informed that I can only be accompanied by one family member. I say no because I need my family close to me, who currently are taking turns sitting by my side to tell me more wretched stories. Instead, I opt to remain in Lusaka with the extended family until Professor Mulla can make the decision to let me fly.

Finally, the plane arrives one afternoon and I choose Notulu to accompany me on my evacuation trip. On that December day, we leave Zambia on an air ambulance arranged by the African Medical Research Foundation (AMREF)[5]. We fly to Nairobi where I am transferred onto a British Airways flight to London Heathrow. During the layover in Nairobi, my friend and Zambian High Commissioner to Kenya, Ambassador Brenda Muntemba, comes to the airport and waits in the air ambulance with me. She weeps uncontrollably and I soon find myself comforting her and telling her the 'remember that time when' stories. Oh Brenda, my darling Brenda. I survived and you did not. This should have been our story.

My survival was made possible by a man I do not know, and who I have not met since. I pray that, one day, I will find that unknown taxi driver – my hero. I pray for the opportunity to meet him and say, 'Thank you'. I never knew his name, and I doubt he ever told it to anyone. I don't even know if anyone gave him money to clean the bloodstains I left in his car that day. Not only did he show wonderful kindness and humanity, but he also risked all he had to save the life of a stranger. I sincerely pray God shows him favour in his life and in his family. I can never thank him enough. I owe him a special debt of gratitude.

'It's funny how, in this journey of life, even though we may begin at different times and places, our paths cross with others so that we may share our love, compassion, observations, and hope. This is a design of God that I appreciate and cherish.'

Steve Maraboli[6]

CHAPTER THREE

MOUNTAIN PRAISE

'I know the master of the wind; I know the maker of all things. He can calm down the winds and make the sun to shine again. Jesus is the maker of all things. He is the maker of that leg, and I still believe Him as a miracle-working God. He remains the doctor of all doctors. Mwangala, say Amen with me.'

Patrick M. Nswana

I am of the belief that there is no higher authority than God to whom I can plead my case, and therefore, the logical assumption is to use my direct line to Him and I make the call.

'Lord, give me but a brief moment, so you can hear my plea.'

'I know the master of the wind; I know the maker of all things,' says the voice inside my head.

'Patrick, I recognise your voice. I'm trying to call God, could you put the phone down so I can get through?'

But instead, I hear Patrick's voice again at the end of the line saying,

'Jesus is the maker of all things. He is the maker of that leg, and I still believe Him as a miracle-working God.'

'Patrick, please, I'm begging you, put down the phone. I need to speak to God and you're keeping the line busy,' as I plead with him further.

However, when the conversation ended, I am disappointed to find that time did not stand still for me. It is the eve of the night before my operation and all my energy has been spent on trying to negotiate with God, through Patrick, who has insisted on hoarding the line, using every possible skill that I possess.

I am not *Neo*, the superhero in *The Matrix*, able to dodge bullets in a backward anti-gravity bend. Instead, in my time of crisis, I am left with no body armour, drowning in my calamity. My time is running out before the inevitable happens, and I am running out of promises to make and pledges to give. I have made all sorts of promises I am not sure I can keep, but they feel and seem genuine to me, at that time. Then further promises of 'Lord I will do this' to 'Lord I will do that', and with the onset of fear it changes to, 'Lord, I'm sorry, and I'm even more sorry for when I did not know that I should have been sorry.'

This is how my negotiations have been going on all night about what I will do, how I will be a better person, how I will not skip Church, how this, how that, and how I will work for His glory – all night I have prayed, pleaded and pledged. I have cried out to my God to take away the mountain on my shoulders and have begged that the diagnosis be changed to a miraculous healing of sorts, that Patrick, a firm believer in the Faith, is also holding onto. *'And when you pray, do not heap up empty phrases as the Gentiles do, for they think that they will be heard for their many words,'* (Matthew 6:5-7). If only He would save my leg. *Please Lord, don't let them amputate my leg, please don't let them do it.'* 'Therefore I tell you, whatever you ask in prayer, believe that you have received it, and it will be yours,' (Mark 11:24). I have prayed, and all my promises in this moment are authentic to me. I am certain my requests are being heard and God will deliver me because He has given me both condition and promise. There is no doubt my prayers are from my heart and are genuine, but with nothing to settle and no compromise to be made, all that is left is desperation. So, I ponder upon the question of whether I am a believer or a Gentile. I realise now, more than ever, that praise is easier when you are on the mountain top, but in the valley, praise is suddenly the hardest thing to come out of your mouth.

The nurses understand my desperation and respect my need for privacy.

'Mwangala, press the call button if you need me,' says my night nurse as she lowers the volume on the monitors, that pick even the slightest change in my blood pressure. Each outburst of tears causes the monitors to oscillate between bleep, bleeeeep, bleeeep, to a rapid bleep, bleep, bleep, bleep, even though I am in no immediate danger.

Soon, it is 4am and the porters are wheeling me toward the operating room. Laura, the angel nurse who has stood by me since I arrived in England and is now my friend, is silently holding my hand as she guides the bed through the double doors of the fluorescent-lit corridors. It is rather disorienting with my head facing the other direction, and the gurney going in all directions while being pulled and pushed like the stubborn trolleys in supermarkets that have wheels with minds of their own. We come to a stop and I make a final plea to the doctors.

'Please do not amputate my leg when you find that it has been healed.' I am now relying on God's promise.

'It hasn't healed overnight, Mrs Lethbridge,' one of the doctors says, and the certainty of his declaration is clearly marked by the expression on his face.

'I know you think it hasn't been healed, but I have prayed for healing and all I am saying is that, when you find that it *has* been healed, please don't take my leg,' insisting as a declaration of faith more than anything else.

'Okay, *if* it is healed, we will not amputate, but it is not. We don't just amputate people's legs, Mrs Lethbridge. We have tried everything to save your leg, and this is the best way to save your life,' as he tries to reassure me.

I am caught between logic and faith wondering which I should believe. After all, I have prayed, and God must have heard my prayer. He would not let me lose my leg even if the doctor says otherwise. *'What a heathen he must be for not believing in my miracle, but just you wait and see, my leg has been healed,'* I am thinking, willing myself not to say my thoughts out loud. My faith is so strong, believing God has healed me because I am now resting in His promises.

I believe faith is a personal matter, and our personal convictions tell us that God answers our prayers because we make promises and hold them against Him to fulfil. We quote scripture that comforts us in our supplications, believing we must receive what we have asked for because the Bible tells us so. Yet, the same God who heals the faithful also heals the unfaithful. I try to rationalise my belief in the last moments before my ordeal.

The nurse soon comes and requests me to confirm the signature on the form. I nod my head as confirmation and tears roll down my cheeks towards my trembling lips. I do not mind that she can see my ugly crying because there is no room for appealing optics in this situation. It is incomprehensible that my whole life is about to be turned upside down. Therefore, how do I express my true feelings when asked to accept who I will be from this day onwards?

'Mrs Lethbridge, I need you to say it out loudly. Is this your signature, and do you understand the procedure we are carrying out today?' as the doctor continues to gently but firmly obtain my verbal confirmation.

My mind is racing, but there is nothing else I can do, and I nod my head again. I fail to voice my agreement, and with a gentle smile, he asks again but, very slowly this time.

'Mrs Lethbridge, is this your signature?'

The tears are now running freely from eyes and even more slowly than the doctor, I say, 'Yes, it is,' in a mumbling voice.

'What are we doing today?' he prods gently.

The thought of what they are about to do rips my insides apart, but I have to speak if they are to carry on with the task of taking away a part of me. My heart aches.

'You're amputating my right leg,' I say with visible pain on my face.

Another doctor walks in and asks the nurse to show him the marked leg to be amputated. He is satisfied that all the markings are in the correct place and he scribbles some notes in my file. The anaesthetist attempts to place the mask over my face, and I put my hand out to stop him.

'Wait, I need to finish crying,' I plead.

Suddenly all the emotions I had pent up come to the surface like a flash flood and I attempt make one final phone call.

'Hello? Lord? Can you hear me? I am at your mercy, please don't let them take away my leg.'

'Jesus is the maker of all things.'

'Patrick please, am begging you. Put the phone down.'

The doctor's slight squeeze on my hand brings me back to earth.

'It's okay, we're not in a hurry,' he says with a reassuring tone in his voice.

The casual chatting amongst the nurses provides me with some much-needed relief, as they continue with their preparations for the procedure, but it does not alleviate the helplessness I feel. I have resigned myself to what is about to happen and whisper to the anaesthetist that I am ready.

The first doctor finally lets go of my hand and the needle pinches my skin. The burning sensation of the anaesthesia courses through my vein on the back of my hand as he slowly pushes the syringe. I observe their processes of preparation with traces of guilt and shame. I have nothing to say, and I have nothing further to ask, so, lying there staring into space, with a crippling heartache, I withdraw from the reality of the final episode playing out in my own series and instead, relive 'McDreamy's' last scene. I drift off wondering whether this is what he felt when he lay there helplessly, urging the doctor not to do this, not to do that, unable to talk but knowing that he would surely die… *Am I seriously crying for 'McDreamy'?* But my volume of tears is interrupted when I feel the clasp of the name tag on my left hand, which instantly brings me back to the present.

'Mrs Lethbridge, please count for me?' says the anaesthetist.

I am not thinking of the numbers themselves in their serial order or in any mathematical way, but I count them stoically:

'One, two, three, four…' and just before I drift off into a deep sleep, in a distressed voice, I manage a final whisper.

'Patrick, call God for me. I couldn't get through.'

'But I am hurt and in pain, give me space for healing in mountain air, let me shout God's name with a prayerful song; let me tell of His greatness.'

Psalm 69:29-30

CHAPTER FOUR
CULTURAL DILEMMA

'So long as you remain blindly obedient to your own culture, other cultures would always remain as "other" cultures.'

Abhijit Naskar – Build Bridges not Walls: In the name of Americana[7]

Supporting patients to maintain their hygiene needs while in hospital is a fundamental aspect of nursing care.[8] Whilst bathing is a well-known relaxation technique and perhaps a healer of body and mind, in hospital I found it to be a confusing and stressful time. My independence was gone and as for my dignity, well, I tried hard to hold onto the little that was left. The nurses, in Zambia, had fallen into their own routine. I did not specifically request for it, but it is what it is, and I am grateful for it.

The female nurses give me sponge baths while the male nurses administered my medication. Uninhibited, as I deem myself to be, the traditional African context where gender roles are ill-defined is partly how I was raised by my maternal grandmother, but fortunately, my parents raised us with modern concepts of gender roles. *Superman* can be a woman they said, and no, not *Wonder Woman* but *Superwoman*. In ordinary circumstances, my modern ways would take precedence, but in this instance – even for an open-minded person like myself – I fail when I am put to the test as the tenets of the medical profession do not segregate based on gender.

My risk-seeking brother, who in his younger years was the black sheep of the family, had once told me that the trick to lasting the weekend in a Zambian police cell was to have a water and soup diet the entire weekend. Come Monday, you do your business in the privacy of your home and your dignity remains intact.

I have tried this out the last three days to trick my digestive system; needless to say, it has its limitations, and one finally must do what needs to be done. Although I am in a private room where I can discreetly perform my morning toilet on a bedpan, even with my limited mobility and multiple fractures, it is definitely not an option I want to consider. I have conjured all sorts of images; my stomach has tightened into a knot. I imagine myself to be a strong woman that cannot be compromised. Oh, what ignorant bliss!

I have asked the female nurses to help me move to the toilet, which is across from my bed. With my broken bones and multiple injuries, they have been begging me to stay in bed before I hurt myself further. After much screaming and hollow threats, the nurses have finally obliged, but what follows is one of the most excruciating experiences of my life, which I hope never to relive.

They try to transfer me from the bed to the wheelchair but wherever they touch me, I scream out loud from the pain. I hold onto the cold metal rail of the hospital bed for support and fight the rising panic within me. My stomach is clenched as I quickly suppress a shiver of fear that has developed probably from the combination of pain and anxiety, and although I can feel the lump in my throat getting larger, I am determined to make it to the bathroom. The distance, which is probably no more than a few metres, has taken me half an hour, as I keep requesting for 'just two seconds' to catch my breath. Finally, we make it, what seems like a mile to cross, and I lean back onto the cold cistern for support. The humiliation I tried to avoid earlier now overwhelms me. The dignity I thought I would preserve now becomes an experience I wish I did not live to see. I feel defeated and tired, from what should have been a simple manoeuvre and in what should be seen as a victory.

The nurses excuse themselves to give me some privacy and the tears drop down my face freely. I cover my face with my hands to try and muffle the sobs and groans that have escaped me. I can hear them whispering behind the closed door; they are not mocking me, just talking about my stubbornness and my need to use the bathroom over a bedpan.

'*Ba kazi aba ba vuta*,' whispers one nurse to the other regarding my stubbornness.

'*Ah, ine ba ma ni yofya*,' says the other, stating how fearful she finds me.

'*Ah, ba vesa chifundo mwandini*,' says the first nurse, who seems to have finally felt sympathetic towards my predicament.

Any other day, I would have laughed, but today, I am crying. It is all too much for me and I am overwhelmed by the lightning bolts of pain going through my body. I still myself to allow the bolts to subside into thuds. What used to be an ordinary task for me has suddenly become a process that requires calculation and willpower to achieve. How is it that I cannot move myself unless I have someone to help me? How is it that what I had done naturally as a matter of course without much thought all my life has become an issue of whether I will fall and hurt myself? I no longer have control of my personal activities. All these conversations with myself and my heightened emotions cause my body to shut down. The trek across the room has become pointless and now we need to do that all over again to get me back to the bed. I dread what lies before me as I look at my legs that were carefully raised onto a chair to maintain their straight form and my gaze is fixed steadily onto the metal pins that stick out of my bandages. I feel *grim* at the thought of the nurses accidentally touching one of the pins, like a knife scratching a plate or the sound of fingernails on a blackboard. I take a deep breath, call out to the nurses to say I am ready, and close my eyes.

In many ways, the UK hospital is no different from the Zambian one. The routines are the same – sponge bath in a soapy basin. Instead of coming out clean, I am left feeling sticky and smelling of soap, which might have been the objective.

Laura, the Spanish nurse with a youthful demeanour, cares for me and gives me the sponge baths, and as I grow comfortable with her – woman to woman – it doesn't seem like a big deal anymore. What began as a patient/nurse relationship has now developed into a strong friendship, but Laura's day off has come and there is only Alberto to give me the sponge bath. What the heck!

Alberto, also Spanish, with slow, deliberate moves full of compassion, is the most familiar with me, and we have talked endlessly about this and the other, especially the fact that, when we first met, I had both my legs. I find refuge in his presence for he tries his best to make me come to terms with my brokenness without forcing me into it. Yet, when it came down to him being the one to give me the sponge bath, I adamantly refuse to be bathed by him. So, there it is again, the cultural monster sitting on my shoulder like the growing orange orangutan I have seen on a particular TV advert that needs to be fed fried chicken constantly to reduce its burden on the shoulder of the one carrying it. But there is not enough fried chicken to get this cultural dilemma burden off my shoulders. Instead, I ask Alberto to set up the basins and soap for me on the adjacent table, declaring that I will do it unaided. I cannot negotiate on this cultural aspect no matter the professional etiquette. My open-mindedness remains tightly shut, and he looks at me comically.

Then he asks, 'How will you do that with only one arm?'

'Go away,' I say to him, and we both burst into comfortable laughter because he knows he will not convince me otherwise. A few minutes later, I call out his name; 'Alberto! Alberto! Help! I can't do it.'

The door quickly opens and there stands a beaming Alberto, who had not gone too far.

'Honestly, Mwangala, I am a nurse, and I'm here to look after you. Just forget about everything and allow me to help you,' he says as he walks in.

I simply nod my head and pass him the facecloth. I must set aside my ingrained beliefs and submit to what is best for me. He maintains his professional decorum in spite of our familiarity. Where my health is concerned, what he represents is an institution of professional care, not friendship. All the banter and jokes do not interfere with his work or professionalism, but he accords me the chance to try it out on my own to see whether I can have the independence I seek. He is available when I call for help and he guides me. This reminds me that, before he is my friend, he is my nurse and caregiver.

Despite what I perceive to be a lost battle, I am determined to win the war. 'Burn the ships,' they say, and I am doing just that as I did in Zambia, insisting on being taken to the toilet across the room. I need to regain as much of my independence as I can, and I have begged so hard that they realise it is pointless trying to convince me otherwise. They carry and place me carefully on the bowl until this becomes the norm. The leg with the metal pins sticking out has been amputated, taking the grim feeling away with it.

Six weeks later, the physiotherapy team comes to my room to give me my first lesson on how to use the commode; how to move out of bed and sit on the contraption. 'Press this button, raise your bed slightly higher and use gravity to gently lower yourself onto the commode,' they say. I move easily and place myself in the correct position, and they gasp in joy and shock.

'How did you manage to do that so easily without any help?' one of them asks.

I explain to them how refusing to use bedpans and insisting on being taken to the bathroom, which incidentally involved me sliding off the bed, may have helped.

'Well, that's lesson one done and dusted,' she says as the team leave giggling and cheering me on.

Finally, there it is – an achievement. I smile to myself, as my resolve has helped me in a somewhat painful but good sort of way to regain my much-sought-after independence; a small achievement for most, but a major milestone for me.

When you are as sick and helpless as I have been, a male nurse stops being a male nurse and simply becomes a nurse, and in hindsight, perhaps, the bedpan was not such a bad idea. However, I decide to do what I feel is best for me. I am taking my well-being and mental health in my possession, hence on some days when I reach the limit of my recommended dosage of pain medication, and still feel like I could do with more pain relief, I do not beat myself too much when I suggest we skip the soapy sponge bath routine for that day. I will still be here tomorrow, a little smelly, but here. Surely, that is not such a bad thing.

I have found that trauma has a way of taking a lot away from someone. It allows for much compromise, and sometimes humiliation, resulting from ingrained beliefs of what the roles of men and women are, even in the routines and functions of hospitals. Some sicknesses come and go, but cultural belief is passed on from generation to generation. My dilemma then was, when do I pretend to be emancipated and open-minded, and when am I being downright ignorant? For as long as I can bathe myself, I find no reason or need to find the definition or elaborate upon its significance, at least not for now.

'It's amazing how a little tomorrow can make up for a whole lot of yesterday.'

John Guare[9]

CHAPTER FIVE

MOUNT KILIMANJARO

'Hey Mwangala, I'm sure you will get over it in no time. You're a strong woman. You know it, and we all know it. I am sorry I didn't call you earlier. Frankly, I've always thought of you, but avoided calling you. I didn't want to hear your voice and didn't know what to say.'

Wassim Assad

I have come to understand that there is a thin line between showing sympathy and showing pity. Any kind of accident is in itself traumatic. There are so many questions about why it happened, how it happened, and what could have been done to avoid it. My accident created a sense of guilt and self-blame, as well as damaging my self-confidence. There has been so much change on how I perceive the people I encountered during my recovery process as I was trying to fit into a past world I left behind. Others saw me as 'business as usual', but many simply did not know what to say to me. What do you say? There is no real balance.

I found myself in the position of reassuring my friends and clients that all was business as usual, and it was okay for me to share my journey of what could be the greatest pain of my life with total strangers and family. But I hid behind a façade of false strength because what most people did not realise was that each time someone asked me, 'What happened?' all I could hear was the horrific sound of the impact of metal crushing my bones – Boom! My body responds to the emotional trauma by freezing and I experience a déjà vu moment. My heart races in a panic and I cannot breathe. The time that passes between the question and my response seems like a moment to others, but within those few seconds, the world stops for me for what seems like an eternity. I take a deep breath and calmly explain 'what happened'. Friends, family and sometimes strangers all ask the same question: 'What happened?' I go through the process of explaining the incident and their expressions range from sorrow to pity… and then the same response of, 'Oh shame,' and sometimes the insensitive prolonged drawl, in a strong Zambian accent, of '*Iyeeeeee, too bad!*'

Then there are those who do not know how to respond at all. Their silence is not by any means an indication that they do not feel any of those expressions, but rather it is a loss for words to say exactly what they feel and see. They are filled with compassionate love that words cannot express. They carry the sorrow of something so terrible happening to me, and the pity that comes with the realisation that this is forever, and forever is a very, very long time. I realise that people express sorrow and pain in different ways, and it has no bearing on what I think or feel.

For some people, it is the coping mechanism of their own mortality and the fear they possess of realising it could happen to anyone. But we are all different in our reactions to trauma, to shock, to emotion, which I acknowledge and accept, and I now find myself reaching out to friends that have not known what to say to me in the hope of regaining my own sanity.

Being able to speak with people about all and nothing has brought me to the realisation that they too were probably trying to cope with how they would speak with me and sound normal without offending me. I may have judged them based on my own perceptions, much of which was untrue looking in retrospect, as most people I know do have compassion – they are sometimes unsure how to show it.

It was on one of my many physio sessions, when I saw a gentleman whizz by me in a wheelchair so competently and so effortlessly, that I wondered how he had achieved such a great skill. Sitting there in my wheelchair, I wondered to myself whether I would ever be able to achieve that level of competency and as I was still obsessing over his skill, he came whizzing by again, but this time, I gained the courage to call out to him loudly and quickly enough to draw his attention towards me.

'Excuse me, sir…' in a slightly trembling voice.

He stopped with a broad smile on his face that I could have sworn was disconnected from the broken body in front of me sitting in the *Whizz Mobil*.

'Yes?' he responded, with a contagious broad smile.

'Sorry to bother you, but I was wondering where you got those knee pads from?' I asked him sheepishly, wondering what they really were though my concentration was on his verve for life.

'I really should begin to sell these,' he laughed as he looked down at them as though at a prized possession. I thought I had offended him and immediately began to apologise but he interrupted me and explained how I was the umpteenth person to ask him about his makeshift knee pads.

'They are simply carpenters' knee pads. If you go to any hardware store then attach some shoe inner soles to make them more padded and durable, then *voila!*', he beamed with arms outstretched. We both burst into laughter like old friends.

I never thought I would find something as adaptable as that in a hardware store for an amputee, but I thanked him, and before he left, he asked me *the question*. Without missing a beat, I ran my mouth explaining to him how I had grown so tired of the question, and how it constantly caused me to relive my experience.

He smiled sympathetically and said, 'I have learnt how to deal with *the question*. I make up stories as I go. Starting from the truth to my wildest imagination.'

He continued, 'My favourite one is telling them how the mafia chopped off my legs in a deal gone bad and they leave me alone. But the look on their faces is priceless,' and he lets out a hearty laugh.

I was thrown back with his response but found it absolutely hilarious at the same time. He had found peace in his condition and made light of what was still a heavy reality for me. We laughed as we shared our real stories and speaking with him made me comfortable as he was sympathetic without trying to make sense of the accident. He looked so happy, and yet he was a double amputee and had lost some of his fingers as well. He wore the biggest and brightest smile ever, and the aura around him was that of peace and immeasurable joy, which the scriptures describe as passing all understanding. He spoke of how he had climbed Mount Kilimanjaro as a double amputee, and thereafter had begun to give motivational talks to help other amputees overcome their limitations and challenges. He expressed a zeal and a zest for life that could not be dimmed by any 'tornado'.

Upon seeing the sadness that shadowed our conversation, he proceeded to give me names of organisations that could provide pillars of support. I wasn't sad because he was happy; I was sad because I saw the opportunities I had lost when I had the capability to do them and forgot to be happy when I should have been. I felt sad for so many varied reasons.

'Don't be sad,' he said gently, 'there are people like yourself who have gone through amputations caused by trauma, who may need support and you too can be someone's pillar of strength. Take my card and call me whenever you like.'

I took the card and watched him speed off. Wow! He had climbed Kilimanjaro, something that was on my bucket list when I was in my twenties and never got round to doing. How could I possibly conquer Kilimanjaro with one leg in my late forties when I hadn't climbed it when I had two legs? I was unsure and it seemed far-fetched. The realisation of my limitations deflated me when I was reminded of who I was now. Inasmuch as I was elated in speaking with someone who seemed to have overcome many challenges in a seemingly worse off physical condition than mine, I lacked his mental stamina especially since I was still supplying the drinks to my pity party.

In my twenties, forty seemed like a lifetime away, yet it came and went and here I was in a wheelchair staring at the business card of a double amputee who had scaled the slopes of Mount Kilimanjaro. I took away one thing from our encounter: that the narrative was mine. Ask me *the question* again and I will tell you whatever version of the cross I feel like carrying on that day.

'It is easier to act yourself into a new way of feeling rather than feel your way into a new way of acting.'

G. D. Morgan[10]

PART TWO
DEPRESSION

'Forgiveness is the fragrance that the violet sheds on the heel that has crushed it.'

Mark Twain[11]

CHAPTER SIX

#JUSTLIVE

'Bo Mwangala, every day is a blessing to be happy. It is only until life starts happening does it slightly blemish one's perception of the day.'

Lafontee Lufungulo

I am failing to move forward; I am stuck in my pain, in my misery, in my despondency, and I need to take that one step that no one can make for me. I have been blaming God for all that has happened to me and asking Him 'Why me?' but then I hear a silent, '*If not you, then who?*' Offended by the rationality of the question, I try to reason with God but soon realise it is a futile mission. How can I block out the negativity brewing within me and focus on how I used to be and instead, start fighting to live?

'*Change your attitude, Mwangala, and stop playing victim but take ownership,*' they say. '*Be positive, Mwangala.*' '*You're lucky to be alive, Mwangala,*' and so it went. I take deep breaths, but it does not calm my emotions. Instead, I hang my head in my hands and cry out in frustration for everyone to leave me alone. What I truly need is for everyone to stop with the church philosophies and the positive mantras but allow me to stay here a little while longer in my wretchedness and in my pitiful state.

In hindsight, I must have irritated the world and all in it with all my slogans and what were to me powerful inspirational hashtags that I had memorised over time, to give me that extra oomph – that motivation that fed my craving to live on a high. For an adrenaline junkie or petrol head like me, they all worked at different times depending on the occasion. '*You will win if you do not give up! Live life on the edge! Live, ride, die! Live life full, die on empty!*' with my personal favourite being the biker's hashtag: '*Live, ride, die!*' or so I thought.

My poor mother, constantly nagging me to stop riding and expressing her distaste for it after my brother Nyambe, a fellow biker, had fallen countless times on his Repsol. I remember sitting in the 'tunnel' at Kenneth Kaunda International Airport, in Lusaka, in the middle of the night awaiting a KQ flight to Kampala.

We were all dressed in our 'Chipolopolo' regalia excited to watch Zambia play an away game against the Cranes in an AFCON cup qualifier. It was almost midnight, and the voice of a lady came through the intercom in hushed, inaudible tones saying something about our flight being delayed, but nothing would dampen our spirits. Hours later, we were at our destination. It was almost dawn when my phone rang.

Instinctively, I looked at my wristwatch wondering who could be calling at that hour. It was my brother's friend Ellington.

'Hi, Mwangala, there's nothing to worry about, but Nyambe is in hospital. He fell off his bike on Great East Road.'

I fell to the ground and in between tears, I bombarded him with questions.

'Ellington, how? When did this happen?'

'Yesterday evening.'

'Ellington, I was still in Zambia. Why didn't anyone call me? Why did you let me jump on that plane knowing that my brother was in hospital?'

'Nyambe told us not to tell you because he knew you were travelling and knew that you would have cancelled your flight.' He continued to try to reason with me, to no avail. I cut the line and cried as I imagined a lot of horrendous possibilities that brought no comfort.

That became my brother's last ride and soon his riding was replaced by weekend braais along a beautiful stretch of the Kafue river. His hashtag became, *Live, build, braai!* but that was not for me.

His fall should have been a deterrent for me from my hashtag of *Live, ride, die!* without realising the *die* part of it was not just around the corner, but was coming head on for me on a very straight road. The winding curves of Siavonga, in the Southern part of Zambia, were always the ultimate high for me. The road winding between cliffs on one side and deep valleys on the other.

Each time we approached the curves, taking a bend, and here it comes: it's a right-turning curve, slowly sliding my weight to the right, shoulder tucked in, left knee pulled outwards helping me to hold onto the bike, right knee almost scraping the tarmac, all the while I am counter-steering. And just as it started to straighten out, it was straight into a left curve, and my body shifts to the left side of the bike in an automatic movement that no longer requires thought and I repeat the slides in the opposite direction. As I am smiling in my helmet, Ian goes past me effortlessly, and instinctively I look at my speedometer and wonder how on earth he could pass me at that speed and make it seem insanely simple.

We would stop at a lay-by, take our helmets off, and let out an adrenaline-pumped scream, breathless and exhilarated, and feeling more alive and present in the moment. Riding brought me so much joy and excitement as it was my 'me' time. There was no one reporting the other as to who would not share the X-Box controller or anyone asking me what was for dinner. The only title I carried was 'midlife crisis at its best' and I was loving it. However, I always ensured that I was acting responsibly during this crisis mode and would, therefore, make the usual call to my husband: 'Luvvie, we're in Siavonga. We made it okay,' and I would get the same response each time: 'Okay babe, see you later. Have fun.' I sit back enjoying my Kariba bream, Ian already cooling himself off in the swimming pool. The occasional warm breeze flowing in from across Lake Kariba is dry and hot. Nevertheless, with eyes closed, I take in a deep breath and my lips curve in a wistful little smile at first, but broaden as joy tugs at the corners of my lips as I relive the sensation of riding through the curves.

However, in trying to move forward, it is the last ride, where I am smiling and then see the car turn into my lane, that I relive. In that moment, everything I have learnt about how to handle myself and my bike is gone. Instead, I hold onto the bars tightly, my legs feel heavy… and I freeze. I do not swerve; I do not stop as per my countless lessons on how to handle an unexpected incident. I simply freeze. I close my eyes and I wait for it. Then I hear it – the sound I have come to understand as the sound of my body breaking and becoming crippled by the emotion that has overpowered me. Fear.

'I have lost my mind in spells and I do not dare to think what I may do in those spells. May God forgive me, and I hope everyone else will forgive me even if they cannot understand. My position is too awful to endure, and nobody realizes it. What an end to a life in which I tried always to do my best.'

Lucy Maud Montgomery

CHAPTER SEVEN

ROCK BOTTOM

'Even if you were completely paralysed from the neck down, one look of disapproval from you would have me quaking in my boots! You have always been and will always be one of the strongest and (in the best possible way) most terrifying people I know, and nothing will ever change that. You may have lost part of your leg, but you still have your mind.'

Jane Scanlon

As generally happens, there is a place that is lower than rock bottom, another layer which is way lower than what my limited mind had imagined. There is not a fair description that can describe my feelings when all my emotions drag me lower into the dark, horrible places I never imagined existed within me. For the most part, rock bottom is loosely identified as depression, just one word – depression: but I have realised there are various degrees of depression, from finding no pleasure in living to uncontrolled hysterics. Gloom wraps a prickly blanket around me and keeps pulling me deeper and deeper into a black hole. Images and memories of my past and present are refreshed every minute of every day, and the days begin to merge into each other, making me lose my will to live in the process.

There is no single degree of depression that can be assigned to such a colossal, overwhelming dread that cannot be described even when you are living with it. Depression does not make a public announcement about its arrival, and neither is there a warning that sounds off to alert you of its presence. It creeps in stealthily and begins to eat at your joy. Anything and everything that represented happiness for me began to fade and lost significance. I detached myself from the people I knew to be the pillars of my existence because I assumed that I was a burden to them and was better off alone. Nothing mattered anymore except the pain I felt deep inside, which could not be reached by drugs or my fingers as I tore at my chest to rip it open and pull it out. However, I felt its presence and it was not going anywhere.

After being discharged from hospital, I have had to undergo various stages of physiotherapy. With my below-knee right leg amputation, I have asked the physiotherapist for crutches because I have seen other amputees 'walking' on crutches, so why not me?

The therapist explains to me that there is a note on my file that disallows the use of crutches because my right arm no longer has capacity to handle the pressure and would cause further injuries if used; but there is another layer of complications because I had been in a lying position for a long period whilst in hospital, which caused weakness in the muscles – meaning the physiotherapy sessions will take much longer than I had expected. *Why not just kill me now*? Hearing this has made me lose the desire to continue with physio because it seems hopeless trying to convince them that my sanity and freedom are dependent on my ability to move independently.

The doctor instead says, although I feel okay, and maybe even feel like 'running', it is time to accept my life as having changed, and I need to give myself and my body a chance to heal. I have suffered a great trauma and am at risk of having deep vein thrombosis, pneumonia, and many other infections too many to mention or understand because my immunity has taken a beating. That is another layer of complication. I feel fatigued from all these arguments and negotiations, and the only thing I genuinely want is to go back home – home where I believe I have a greater chance of regaining my sanity, which I am losing in all this craziness, and that precious freedom has been taken away from me.

I try to foolishly argue that I am HIV negative; therefore, my immunity should be good.

He smiles and says to me, 'Immunity is a lot more than your HIV status, Mwangala.' Well, I am from Africa, what is he talking about? In popular perception, there is correlation between HIV and immunity, but evidently, I have revealed my selective ignorance because really, I know better than that. However, I am in a position where I will say anything to try and convince him to give me my 'get out of jail' card, but he will not. His professional opinion is paramount regarding my wellness and safety. Yet, despite everything that is good about it, the UK suddenly feels like my jail and I want to go home. Another layer of the myriad of complications I do not want to deal with.

This unwanted demon begins to creep into the void where my heart once was, crawling, gnawing from within as the frustration from being told I need to be more patient, that my body needs time to heal, and so it continues to creep in very slowly, occupying a space it does not belong in – this measured approach has me blinded to the effects it is having on my family and the people around me. I am so engrossed in my world of pain, anxiety, and frustration that I do not see what is happening to those that want to help and be there for me. The UK is my new home, but I want to be back in my old home in Zambia, where I delude myself that peace will be found and finally this demon will be exorcised.

I want to feel the warmth of my African sun and the mingled smells of fresh vegetation, the earthy scent from the first rains falling onto dry hot soil, and the aroma of *Mongu* rice waiting to be served. I want to feel I am okay in spite of the trauma I have gone through, and to feel the presence of God in the comfort of my native home: but I am in my English home where my living space has been professionally and immaculately transformed into a recovery ward setting to make me clinically comfortable. The effect of my being downstairs and my husband and the children sleeping upstairs has amplified my aloneness even when I have people with me. I can feel the strain this arrangement has had on my husband's sleep routine with having to run up and down the stairs in the dead of night to help me with the commode, and more so, on the children because now they really do not know how to relate with me. Another wretched layer of frustrations and complications.

Adam and I got married on a blissful morning in a rural setting in my parents' backyard. Like all newlyweds, we had promised each other the world and were determined to raise our children with values that we and they would be proud of. We had what I would call a happy home: Sunday lunches, school plays and the loud extended family we both loved. We did not care about the constant power cuts and the load shedding that affected everyone in the country and yet the feeling of being home could not be traded for anything else in the world. We purchased a family burial plot, which solidified our desire to grow old in Zambia. So, it came as a shock when out of the blue, Adam shared his desire to go back *home*.

'But this is home,' I protested.

Though conflicted by his declaration, it was only fair to give it a shot. UK was a huge adjustment for the family, but we were fortunate enough to find good schools for the kids, a great neighbourhood with the best neighbours possible: Christmas family dinners on the street, cocktail evenings, lots of gin and tonic, and lots of laughter. However, my work had me making long and expensive commutes between the UK and

Zambia, but I traded in my profits for pockets of happiness that left me connected to my country – the place I called *home*.

It was during one of these commutes that I heard the sound; that of my body breaking. My whole world in that single moment was turned upside down leaving me feeling short-changed out of my pocket of joy. Naturally, the doctor's news of the impossibility of travel to Zambia because of my injuries meant my hopes were dashed. I became angry and resentful.

I have not only lost my option to travel but have lost my leg as well. Slowly, I lose all but one of my clients. The world did not stop for me, nor does it wait for anyone. I am angry not only with my condition but also with God. The 'Lord, how could you do this to me?' factor has come into play again and I cannot shake it off despite the many things I should be grateful for. The overwhelming feeling of despondency and hurt has overshadowed my sense of being. I want to end my pain in any way I can, and everyone around me knows the type of words they need to say to encourage me, but they do not encourage me at all: 'Oh, how strong you are' and 'How amazingly you are handling this' or 'God is the healer'. Despite all that they say, what I feel is immeasurable pain from His abandonment, and no, I am not that strong and no, I do not think I am that amazing.

The nagging thought that constantly runs through my mind is to simply end it all. I always thought God was strange and I think to some extent, sometimes unfair. I have begun to question Him on many things these past months because the Bible I read says He (God) does not give you more than you can handle: *but Lord, is it possible that your scale was incorrect when you apportioned my weight of trauma*? It is here, when death beckons, that I have found the layer that is lower than rock bottom.

The wind howling outside, and everyone sound asleep upstairs, I lie alone in my darkened room downstairs and reach over to pick the all-too-familiar bottle of morphine. The dark shadow covering me has silenced everything, and my thoughts hear only one voice: everything has to end. I need to release everyone from the anguish and pain I have imposed onto them. My phone vibrates on the nightstand and instantly startles me and breaks my monologue.

It is my daughter. She is crying and asking to see me.

'Mummy, are you awake?'

'Yes, Nina.'

'Can I come downstairs to talk to you?'

I glance at my watch and it is 2am. I stare at the phone, then at the bottle in my hand, and I quickly turn the cap back on to close it and place it back on the table.

'Yes, Nina.'

What preoccupied my mind a few minutes earlier is quickly realigned to deal with my daughter who now takes pre-eminence over all else. All my thoughts are shifted to what she could possibly want to talk about at this hour.

'Mummy there's this girl at school…?' and she carries on.

She talks about everything that's been going on with her, which I have been oblivious to because my mind has been preoccupied with ending everything. In this present moment, all that does not matter because she is the most significant and highest thought I have now – and as she leaves a couple of hours later, I have only one thought that brings a smile to her face and the solution to the next day's *Mean Girls* drama at her school. *Lord, my daughter still needs me*, I say to Him that knows me well. *My daughter needs her mother.*

I drop my head and begin to cry quietly in despair, frustrated that God could not even grant me the luxury to depart from my brokenness in peace. Certain that I had the choice to do as I pleased, I began to question God's plans for my life.

What may seem like my right to choose does not necessarily mean it is God's choice when He has unfinished business with me. I have hit lower than rock bottom and I cry out to Him once more: *Lord, can you not hear my cries? Why have you turned your face away from me?*

The Old Testament book of Isaiah 38:2-4 saw Hezekiah cry out to the Lord as he turned his face toward the wall and prayed to the Lord. His sickness was not healed, but his life was extended when God answered his prayer through Isaiah to apply a poultice from a lump of figs that was placed on his boil. I feel betrayed because it feels in my heart that God has turned His face away from me. *Why heal Hezekiah and not me? Did I not cry out loud enough or long enough for you to hear me? Did I not turn my face toward the wall as he had done? Is Hezekiah's God not my God? Lord, why have you turned your face away from me?* I have so many questions and I feel so much sorrow, and repeatedly, I ask the Lord: *Why me?* Then, finally, devoid of all emotion, sleep finds me at the layer lower than rock bottom.

'Worry does not empty tomorrow of its sorrow. It empties today of its strength.'

Corrie Ten Boom[12]

CHAPTER EIGHT

SHAME

'Kina hape wa hesu. Kapa uka katala ni na? Kuna kulukile. Kapa u ka ikutwa kuli ni ku sinyeza nako? Kuna kulukile. Ni lapela kuli muni a bupilo habe niwena hau lila, ni hau ikutwa buinosi. Mwa litapelo ni mwa tabo, nikupa kuli utiye. Hani ku libali mulikani. Ni teni. Ka lilato.'

Inonge Lifanu

Shame – that is the only feeling I have each day when I wake up and catch a glimpse of myself in the mirror, such tremendous shame. Each day was planned meticulously. I planned for my life and that of my family and my business with every contingency I could think of. Careful to plan all possible risks and countering them all with backup plans, and backup plans for the backup plans. Yet, the one thing that eluded my foresight, and that I had no backup plan for, was the life-changing loss of my limb.

There is no backup plan for God's plan for my life. But rather than praising Him, I am filled with rage and at the same time feel a sense of loss and absolute shame. I am flawed and undeserving of His grace. What god can validate such a traumatic action to prove a point? I cannot shake off the turmoil of emotions and despondency that I feel, so I clothe myself in this veil of shame, which hides me from my disgrace.

The doctors come and go about their morning routinely rounds. Same questions and I give the same predicted responses. Instinctively, my eyes close when they uncover the sheets that 'hide' my wounds to examine the stump where my leg used to be. The psychotherapist uses his library voice to whisper something to the specialist and when all is done, with exaggerated smiles, off they go. I watch the door close behind them, making sure they have all left before I pour out my grief in a flood of uncontrollable tears.

After the amputation, I reached out to massage my foot as I had usually done before, except this time I touched an empty space on the hospital sheet. I was experiencing phantom pain. Laura and Alberto, the nurses looking after me, then assumed the additional role of 'shrink' by suggesting that I look at my *missing* limb in the mirror as an attempt to trick my brain or recondition it into accepting the change in my physiology. An overly excited Alberto was eager for me to try out what he had been reading the previous night on the technique. They worked with me to ease the pain using the 'mirror trick' as a mental adjustment to help in the reconditioning of my brain. Phantom limb pain is a mental phenomenon that I have to adjust to.

For some people it works, for others it does not. As Sod's law would have it, I am the 'some people' for whom it does not work. Strong-minded as I used to be, how could I fight and conquer something that is phantom in nature? Another way in which I felt God showed His sarcasm as a reminder of His Omnipresence.

Finally discharged from hospital and attempting to settle into regular home routines, I am reminded constantly that my leg is missing. The door openings are not wide enough for the wheelchair, so I prefer to lie in bed. I wake up in the middle of the night and I roll to my side to put my foot down, again I am reminded that I have lost the tiny privilege of being able to hold my bladder until the very last minute to maximise on my sleep before rushing to the toilet, because I can no longer reach the floor. I press the internal intercom that has been installed in the house and ask my husband to come downstairs to help me. Failing to perform ordinary tasks such as this is not an easy adjustment, and then suddenly, the shame is overwhelming. I crawl back into bed and pray for darkness to come, but it does not come soon enough – it is only 5am.

Catherine, my prosthetist, tries to convince me that I will see myself differently and in a more optimistic manner once I receive my prosthesis. I hold my tongue to avoid being rude to this wonderful person trying her best to help me. The question, however, lingers on my mind. Did you save my leg? Are you the angel I have been waiting for to burst through my door shouting, 'Taa-daaa! Just joking, here's your leg. I hid it.' The thought of having my leg back and erasing everything that happened in between is something I have prayed and hoped for. Thoughts of carrying on with my life without my leg makes me feel incomplete and damaged. I cannot imagine my life without my leg – I just can't. Instead, I simply smile and nod my head in agreement because she does not seem to understand my fear – the fear I have and moreover, my shame.

Close your eyes, Mwangala.

*

I am in Zambia with my parents and dad has just cracked a joke. As usual, I am the only one that has found it funny and my eyes water from my side-splitting laughter. My mother grunts in disapproval and walks off. Then I am with Usha having lunch but my smile quickly turns into a frown as I try to recall whether or not where we are is wheelchair friendly – I'm an architect and I cannot recall such an important detail, I feel even more shame. Where will Usha and I have lunch now? The sound of the phone ringing disrupts my mental journey and it is my sister Notulu.

'Hi Noti.'

'*Bo* Mwangala, today you were my subject of discussion at my book club meeting. We read the book *Who Moved My Cheese?* You are the one person I thought of who has always been ready with running shoes tied around their neck. I shared with the group how even while you were in recovery, my first business-class trip overseas was because of you. You gave us access to five-star vacations using your time-shares. At your worst, you were able to provide your best for all of us. I said to them, you cannot move my sister's cheese as she will never be without a backup plan. Your whole life you prepare backup plans, and your shelf is filled with books to feed your brain with relevance, and we teased you about it. I was not bragging, *Bo* Mwangala. I realised as I shared with the club, that you are my prime example of what that book is about.'

'Noti, can I call you back?' is all I manage to blurt out before cutting the line.

I take a deep breath to control the lump in my throat and slowly exhale.

'Lord, I did not have a backup plan for this. I did not have a backup plan for the shame that I feel.'

'God's priorities for efficiency in this life are not ours... Frustrating human efficiency is one of God's primary means of sanctifying grace.'

Pastor John Piper[13]

CHAPTER NINE

FIRST TIME SINCE

'Everything can be taken from man, but one thing: the last of the human freedoms – to choose one's attitude in any given set of circumstances, to choose one's own way.'

Viktor E. Frankl[14]

Today is the first time since that day. So many 'first times' since that day that I can't wait to finish the list of 'since that day' for each day to slowly become the norm. The many 'first times since' experiences are things I took for granted and did without much thought, yet after experiencing a traumatic event, they seem novel. Ordinarily, such things would neither have mattered nor registered with me, yet here I am now looking at everything as though they are something new, and the list is endless with the only new norm being the sleep disorder I have developed resulting from fear.

My sessions with the therapist do not have the couch, but there is the large box of tissues on the coffee table that I've never used, and it is the same story each time I visit. Not once have I cried during these sessions because I act brave, hoping I will be told I am okay and finally get the 'get out of jail' card I covet.

'Doc, please say I'm okay so I can go home. I want to go home,' I say, but I get the same response from him.

'But you are home. Why Zambia? Who is in Zambia?' he asks me in the hope that I would give a different response this time that would influence his decision to grant me parole.

I exhale deeply because I know he will not understand anything I say, but seeing I am in a safe space to speak candidly, I let it all out.

'Doc, it is not *who* is in Zambia; it is *what* is in Zambia. It is my veranda that overlooks the dambo. It is my dogs that chase the birds every morning and the therapeutic motion of watering my lawn each morning, the endless cups of tea, and the view of the sunset along the Mongu-Kalabo road. It is the happiness I feel when I am there. Zambia is home because it is where I am happiest, where we were happy as a family,' and without warning I break down into uncontrollable gut-wrenching sobs.

For the *first time since*, I weep, and instead of sectioning me as I had feared, he has declared that we have finally made progress.

Smiling warmly, he says, 'Okay, now, we are getting somewhere. So, I suggest you cry some more.'

This is not what I expected but I look up through my teary eyes and laugh at his advice with great relief. What initially felt like a burden is suddenly not there anymore. Somehow, the unburdening and expression of my emotions and thoughts has lifted a weight off my shoulders. I am speaking with a person who is not judging me but seeking to help me find myself in all the craziness and guilt I feel. I felt selfish for wanting so badly to go back home to Zambia and feared voicing it out to my husband or family members. It does not seem so bad now that I have told someone who is unrelated to me.

After the session, I have newfound courage and say to my husband, 'Adam, let's go home.'

'But this is home too,' he responds, and I see his puzzled face considering this was supposed to have been a settled matter.

'Yes, there are great advantages here as the healthcare is amazing, and the kids are getting a good education, but we have lost our laughter. We have lost our inner peace, and we are losing our love,' I try to justify my reason without imposing my desire.

While the social environment has presented us with all that we need, the loss of laughter and inner peace seems to be too much of a sacrifice to bear. I want to have that laughter, joy, and peace back in my Zambian home which I am not experiencing in my UK home. It is the first time since that day that I have verbally said I want to go back home, but it is also the first time since that I have not lost my temper unnecessarily when the kids ask me for the same thing twenty times after I said the first 'no'. It is the first time that I am empathetic toward my husband because he is home in his home country, and I should be happy for him. My veranda will always be there, but my babies are growing and soon they will not ask me twenty times over after the first 'no'. Oh, what a dilemma.

I have known the probabilities of this day were high and hoped it would never come, especially when the challenges are presented, and you reach the dreaded crossroad of being in a mixed-culture marriage. Where exactly is home? By its design, marriage comes with its own challenges irrespective of the cultural imbalances, but when cultures are intertwined, there can be a double portion of challenges that need to be addressed. Home can soon be a hurdle based on how it is defined within your marital context. People say home is where your heart is, but where exactly is that? My definition of home and my husband are similar yet different. Our perspectives of what makes us happy are individual yet collective. I need to feel the happiness I can easily associate with, and Zambia for the moment seems to have the kind of happiness I seek.

I found that the UK was more responsive to people with disabilities as compared to Zambia, and to avoid what felt like a Band-Aid response to my healing, the deep-end challenge of *first time since* soon became replaced by *what if*. The 'What if they…' is beginning to preoccupy my thoughts, and there are so many 'What if' insecurities developing in my mind with the strongest being *What if people laugh at me?* A question only to be resolved if I went back home.

In many ways, I felt guilty for not fully appreciating the care the UK offered, which was far superior to what my own country could offer, so why would I want to spit in the face of a government that was looking after me so well? Naturally, I hide this thought from my English shrink.

The day comes and Zambia is knocking at my door, which I find both nostalgic and daunting. Having departed on an air ambulance, now the return leg (no pun intended) is as a 'special needs' passenger seeking the love and familiar comfort of home. I want so badly to reconnect with my familiar space, smell the fragrances of the blooming flowers in my garden and the African sun on my face. Clara will be so pleased to know I will no longer evade the sun's rays on my face.

The familiar airports I have passed through countless times on regular excursions now seem so different and strange as I am being wheeled through check-in and immigration, and through passages and routes I never even knew were there.

Unable to board the plane like everyone else, the passenger-assist vehicle awaits me. The experience does not make me feel special, instead I feel different and disconnected from the rest of the passengers, but that's fine because finally I am home. Adam meets me halfway and has asked me to give Zambia a trial period of four weeks after which we can go back to the negotiating table.

The drive home through the familiar roads from the airport is bittersweet and seeing the grass brown and scorched from the heat and baking sun with little gardening care, my mind races with comparisons already. The all-too-familiar bicycles laden with bags of charcoal and vegetables on their way to market swerve on and off road as they usually do, which endangers not only their lives, but those of the people who drive on these roads as well. The haphazard placement of billboards – some faded by the sun over the years – reminds me instantly of where I am and still, I smile because this is the place I call home. Everything is mostly unchanged except for a few changes here and there to the landscape and the all-too-familiar police roadblock on the airport road, whose only purpose seems to be to pile up traffic. But its presence even after all these years is a joy to see, especially since it provides a balance for my current chaotic mental state. *Did I just crack a joke?* The corners of my eyes crease with amusement and I let out a deep exhale.

The first week slowly turns into three weeks of staying indoors, keeping myself away from everyone. I do not know how I should react if they ask me how I'm doing. What do I tell them? How miserable I feel, how my life has been disrupted? Or do I just say how grateful I am that I am still alive? What and how do I feel? I really do not know. So, it is safer to sit on my veranda even though it is not what I envisioned my healing process in Zambia would be like. Avoidance has become my norm, so sitting on the veranda doing nothing but watching the weavers 'destroy' my palm trees to build their nests is easier than addressing the elephant in the room. Every year, the same palm trees, the same nests, and I am very sure it has to be the same weavers, else how would they know where my veranda was? The sight of this positive destruction is a welcome change I have longed for; a familiar experience I have grown accustomed to.

'Enough is enough,' Lungowe my sister declares almost angrily, 'it's time for you to try and meet the rest of the world.'

Indeed, people are talking and most do not disguise their stares. I could not handle it and demand to be taken straight back to my veranda where I sink into a depressive state. The ultimate Sod's Law must be being rejected by the country I so much yearned for. I blame God for not answering my prayer as it seems easier to blame someone that does not talk back. Everything is taking a toll on me and as I sink further into that crater of desolation, I begin to blame myself for everything that has happened and for the *first time since*, I no longer know where I want to be.

'If you trade your authenticity for safety, you may experience the following: anxiety, depression, eating disorders, addiction, rage, blame, resentment, and inexplicable grief.'

Brené Brown[15]

CHAPTER TEN

MY HEART WILL HEAL

'My friend, always remember, no matter what, keep walking; don't slow down, don't look back, we are here now, and I am walking by your side.'

Dr Usha Padmanabhan

Perfectionist, Obsessive Compulsive Disorder, competitive, focussed, neurotic, difficult, rigid, stubborn and 'verbally violent'. Then, at the very end of the spectrum, was kindness. Terms my family and friends used to describe my personality. I would consult Usha to confirm some of the descriptions I thought were too harsh and she would laugh it off and Clara just gave a half shrug with a hint of 'So what?' at the end. But some of these must have been true because they hindered a vitally important aspect of my recovery. I was more focussed on physical milestones such as how many steps I could take that day, how high I could raise my lifeless arm, how easily I could navigate my wheelchair through a door, than on the most mundane task of finally being able to make my own cup of tea. I did not understand the extent of my injuries, therefore, I made up assumptions to complete my assessment, the neurotic part of me, which naturally was wrong.

There probably was just as much mental as physical damage, if not more. My heart was as broken as my body and it too needed healing, healing that could only come from a point of acceptance – acceptance of my new physical state. It became clear that the waterfall of tears was the outcry of my spirit. The deep state of unforgiveness lay rooted within me, causing intense emotional pain, sorrow and despair. *How could he do this to me? Why didn't he die? Why has his life carried on as if his life is worth more than mine?* All these questions developed a hatred and unforgiveness towards the drunk driver that put me here. My stomach would turn, instinctively, clutching the gold cross hanging from my chain, and as I tried to ease the war within my mind, tears of despondency cascaded down my cheeks leaving me weak and frail. Each heart-wrenching sob was more painful than the last as my mind recreated the scene repeatedly as if I did not want to forget but needed to fuel the unforgiveness and unworthiness I felt. I have not forgiven him, and more importantly, I have not forgiven myself for being here and losing my limb. I have not let go of that shame.

People ask me, 'What happened?' in a rather curious way that seeks some tragic response to explain the ordeal, and my cold response when I say, 'It was a motorbike accident' attracts a pregnant pause that is then followed with the '*Ooooooh*!' in a long drawl and sometimes in a deeply Zambian accented '*Iyeeeeee*', I know what that is and what it means. It is: 'Oh, but people on motorbikes are careless,' and 'Oh, motorbikes are dangerous.' It is, 'Oh, what was a girl doing on a bike anyway?' with the 'anyway' added for extra sarcasm. I know what 'Oh' means, whether it is intentional or not, is subject to speculation, but I have no doubt in my mind what it means.

The Italian Orthopaedic Hospital is built along a beautifully tree-lined avenue in the heart of the capital city and less than a couple of kilometres from State House, the home and offices of the Republican President. A road I travelled along countless times both as a child and as an adult to watch the soldiers smartly dressed in their uniforms and standing in a frozen state at the front of the magnificent-looking gates of State House entrance. But I never gave a second thought to the hospital's presence, which would later play a vital role in my survival.

'Good morning, ma'am.'

I turned my head towards the sound of the voice and saw a uniformed officer standing in the doorway. My mother, who had been sitting at the foot of my hospital bed for the last couple of days, talked to the stranger and a few moments later I heard the familiar slow deliberate footsteps make their way towards me. Upon entering my room, her security detail discreetly disappeared to offer her some privacy. She hugged my mother as they exchanged pleasantries in muffled voices.

The she asked me *the question* with a distressed voice.

'What happened?'

'Motorbike accident,' I said to her with the usual respect I accorded her, but she sought further clarity while suggesting objects that could either amplify or alter my response.

'*Mukwae, neli jinga?*' ('Princess, you mean a bicycle?') she asked in a surprised but, controlled, low voice.

'*Batili*, Honda,' ('No, motorbike') I repeated. I then gave a generic description as I would if I were in rural Zambia where toothpaste is Colgate, washing powder is Surf, and every motorbike is a Honda.

Then she looked at me with a frown and a twisted lip turned at the edge, and I knew what was coming next – I could have put a bet on it. Saying it out as loudly as only she would in her soft-spoken voice,

'*Cwale neuyezani fasinto se si cwalo mukwae?*' ('What were you doing on such a thing?') she questioned me and turned her back towards me. She covered her face with her palm of her hands and began to sob. At first gently, then as her shoulders began to heave up and down, the sobbing intensified, broken only by the occasional, '*mawe mwanake*' (my child).

Call it relief or disappointment, but finally someone had managed to express my paranoia out loudly, and I was glad that she had the courage to say it. It was something I kept inside whenever people reacted in that way but would never show what I felt. But in this instance, I watched her sob as my mother, who was now sitting across the room from me, joined my sobbing aunt in what felt more like the mourning of a lost soul than the preservation of a living being. My heart went out to these two women but at the same time I felt like screaming 'I am not dead yet,' feeling slightly irritated, as I wondered why all elderly relatives do that, but I decided the polite thing to do was to join in the weeping session, just as we all do at funerals regardless of how well (or not) we knew the deceased. I should have felt some sense of relief doing that; little did I know then that I would not stop crying for a really long time after that. Talk about a Pandora's box.

I kept thinking that I should have lost a limb in a more 'meaningful' way where I emerged heroic – meaningful enough to win me accolades of bravery without having to explain myself. Trying to find meaning in explaining or rationalising something so traumatic was meaningless, and instead it had caused me greater pain and did not provide comfort in any way. The fact remained: loss of a limb, irrespective of the circumstances, amounted to the same trauma associated with it. There is no heroic way to losing a limb. I realise very quickly that losing a limb as a result of diabetes is no different from one who loses it from cancer, a road accident or an occupational hazard. The bottom line is that limbs are lost.

Therefore, seeking any other way to solicit acknowledgement did not make the pain or trauma less intense. Forgiving that unknown person who hit into me, sending me into that storm water drain, although vitally important, I could not do until I forgave myself. As much as he was there, at that hour, regardless of his drunken state, so was I.

Usha? How can I keep walking with you now?
Forgive yourself, Mwangala, then, forgive him.
I can't, it hurts too much.
Yes, you can.

'Don't walk in front of me, I may not follow. Don't walk behind me, I may not lead. There is only one happiness in life – to love and be loved.'

George Sand[16]

CHAPTER ELEVEN

NOTHING IS EASY

'Obstacles are those frightful things you see when you take your eyes off the goal.'

Henry Ford[17]

'Good morning, Honourable, how are you?'

'I am good. I just ran fifteen kilometres around Fiji, and mostly, it is because I got lost.'

We laugh.

'But how do you do it at your age when I'm younger than you are by a margin, and I can't even complete a three-kilometre run?'

He lets out a hearty laugh. 'It is not easy, Mwangala; nothing in life is easy,' he says with his comfortable signature smile.

There are so many emotions that I still have to contend with, and being in hospital has its challenges, yet there is more to contend with when I get back home to recover. The Honourable called to check on how I was recovering having maintained our communication since I left Zambia, but when I tell him I have quit physio and will be happier in my wheelchair because the prosthesis hurts my stump each time I wear it for more than thirty minutes, he simply states, 'Don't quit, Mwangala.'

The Honourable MP was an old family friend who always visited me during my hospital days. It was a welcome respite from my pain to talk about politics, to drink tea, and to laugh about all and nothing without once forgetting the severity of the situation. Nonetheless, it was a good distraction from everything I was feeling, especially the uncertainty of my future.

Then another a higher-ranking official comes through, which was a welcome distraction, though with a different level of decorum considering the relationship we have. Her visit resulted in having the ward I was in being cordoned off, which caused warranted curiosity from staff and visitors alike. For security reasons and unknown to me, the ward was closed off to public visits, and for a brief moment, in spite of my pain, I felt like a superstar.

When all was done and dusted, and the superstar status left with the dignitary, it was time for my regular sponge bath and the nurse shyly asked me; 'Madam, who are you?'

I laughed, fully aware what had prompted that question, but decided to play along and cheekily said, 'Three days you have bathed me and still you don't know my name?'

She laughed. 'No, I mean, who are you because *big people* come to see you.'

I knew what she meant by *big people* but maintained my innocence.

'Read my hospital file. My name is on it,' and we burst out laughing.

The few days I spent in that hospital, being dependant on the nurses as I was for every relief, comfort and recovery, helped me understand the magnitude of eternal gratitude. But on days like today having undergone yet another surgery, big people, small people, all people leave me alone. It hurts everywhere.

'Don't quit, Mwangala. I am where I am today, and have gone through so much, and if I had given up each time I was met with a challenge, I would not be here. Nothing is easy. Always remember that. Those were the Honourable's words that I recall and try to draw strength from, but I can't really apply it to myself because I am in physical pain. I struggle to maintain a positive attitude and I whisper to myself, 'Mwangala, nothing is easy.'

His mentorship into my political life before and after the accident has given me the courage and the resilience to withstand most things thrown at me. The accident may have been a curve ball, but his persistence to help me see myself beyond my current situation gives me hope. I had my personal views about the political world, but his mentorship opened channels in my mind I never considered.

I presumed that I had enough intellect to weather any storm until he clearly broke it down for me regarding the enormity of the journey I was embarking on. When my attempt in the political arena failed to yield the fruit I desired, he did not call it failure but a learning curve. He continued to support and mentor me, even when I seemed to have been giving up on my political aspirations, and challenged me to channel my inner strength to my recovery and regain my focus and patriotism. It seemed easier to give up than to keep fighting for my health and ambitions.

What should have been a mere political association turned into a patriotic alliance. He helped me to see myself not only as a political figure, but someone who should be prepared to serve the vulnerable and the marginalised in society. Little did we know at the time that he would one day be championing for my survival. 'Don't quit,' he said, encouraging me to get back to my physiotherapy sessions. Our political ideologies may have been different, but we looked past all those political affiliations and saw each other as compatriots fighting for the same cause.

It has been three days and I haven't got out of bed and I don't want to serve; I simply want to be saved. I am finding it harder and harder with each passing day to keep myself motivated. It seems easier to just lie here and wait for whatever it is I am waiting for. What am I waiting for exactly? A job, a life, a career, 2021 so that I can stand in an election again? What exactly am I waiting for: death? Did the Honourable know, and does Clara know it as well, that it is definitely not easy? Is this my life now and how I will live it? How really do I want to write the story of my life? What should it say? *'She lay there waiting…'* After all these positive affirmations and questions, it is easier to simply roll over and go back to sleep although it is 10am in the morning.

'Sleep, those little slices of death — how I loathe them.'

Edgar Allan Poe

CHAPTER TWELVE

TEAM BEACH

'Mwanake, why do you want to put ramps inside your house, when it is better for you to learn how to walk?'

Clara Mvula

Being in the UK meant that the medical care I needed was available, but it took me away from the larger part of my support system – my *extended* family. I missed the camaraderie and affection so much that when my friend and half-life, Clara, broke the news that she would come to UK just to visit me, I almost went bonkers with joy.

Clara, always affectionate but firm. Always mixing up the friend and the mother roles. Perhaps it's because she was my senior at school, or perhaps it's because she got to have her own home before I did, or perhaps it was simply that Clara loved to be prim and proper, and I definitely indulged her. Why not? After all, I spent most weekends at her flat after she graduated from the Copperbelt University in Kitwe, Zambia. Kitwe, a slow, rumbling mining town, where you were expected to be either a '*Bashi Mine*' or a '*Bana Mine*' that being the ultimate success of being employed by the copper-mining conglomerates that monopolised all things Kitwe.

Clara is the friend that I consider to be my other half – the friend I cry, laugh, and will probably grow old with; the one who brings positive energy into my space.

The day finally came and after a long-haul flight, a tired-looking Clara walked through my bedroom door and gave me a warm bear hug. In difficult times, she and I spoke the same language – the language of comfortable silence, and I couldn't thank her enough on that occasion for understanding my conflicting need for silent company. But after day three of watching me lie in bed, she had had enough.

There was only so much we could reminisce about, and only so many encouraging words that could be spoken, so on day three, she had had enough of my whingeing and…

'Don't let just lying there become comfortable,' she firmly said.

It is a wake-up call for me, but I don't know what needs to be done.

'Enough, Mwangala, I didn't fly halfway around the world to sit on the edge of your bed to watch you drink tea. This is simply not you,' she declares sharply.

I see the frustration in her eyes and even in my helpless state I feel for her, knowing there is not much any of us can do. Her frustrations echoed mine, but I did not know how to get up. I am in this position, but I can't seem to be able to pull myself out of this malaise quickly enough. She has challenged me to try and find my old self in the midst of the turmoil that is going on in my life; easier said than done because it requires tapping into my inner being, acknowledging my disability, seeing the lemonade and not the squeezed lemons on the side. But Cathy Guiswite had it right when she said: 'When life gives you lemons, squirt someone in the eye.' Naturally, I found it easier to be cynical than to declare positive affirmations during the process of denial.

The two weeks that follow are best described as the hardest and most rewarding I have ever had. Under duress, I finally agree to sit in the conservatory, a room I once loved and had spent endless hours in, reading one of my many books on leadership and politics. I stole a quick glance at my abandoned CD player, but I am pleasantly surprised at the warmth of the sun on my face, and for a moment, as I close my eyes, I am reminded of Zambia except in this case sun is kissing my face without scorching it. I shield my face from the sun's rays and I smile because the only blinding light I have seen lately comes solely from the light bulb in my room upstairs. Even for me, it is better than just staying indoors lying on my bed never knowing what the feel of fresh air and blue skies is like.

'What's that smile about?' she asks me, wondering what could have transformed me suddenly from being gloomy to my radiant demeanour.

'Nothing,' I reply as I roll my eyes, pretending not to want to share the experience when, in fact, I was too proud to let her see how this little bit of sunshine on my face has created a huge magical moment within me.

Begrudgingly, I slowly turn towards her to respond to her question, but just as I open my mouth to speak, we are interrupted by the sound of Clara's phone ringing. I let out a sigh of relief and turn my face upwards, towards the magic.

'Hey Joe,' (long pause) 'yes I had a safe trip, and Mwangala is getting stronger,' she says. It is her brother Joe from Cape Town. There is some indistinct mumbling going on for a while, then I hear her say, 'Oh, we're just chilling here with Mwangala's leg', and she bursts into laughter.

The words are spoken in jest and my initial reaction is to take offence because it seems to be my constant disposition lately. But then again, I look at my leg over there and here I am sitting over here and realise that she isn't wrong after all. We were chilling with the leg that I have or the one that I do not – again more *lemony* stuff. Slowly, I sip my umpteenth cup of tea and smile because I see the irony in it and I am feeling happy chilling with my friend. Whether I have one or both legs, it does not seem to rattle her. This is Clara.

Her presence in our home has brought back the laughter that we seem to have placed at the back of the top shelf, right behind the ice cream maker that has lost its novelty, but is kept for the 'Mrs Bouquet' moments of our lives, when we pretend the that the ice cream we're serving at book club is homemade, when in fact, it just came out of a plastic tub purchased from the corner shop and served *a la Mwenda*. But on this Sunday morning, sitting in my wheelchair watching Clara teach Nina how to cook Sunday lunch, something I never found the time to do, there is nothing Bouquet-ish about this moment. I watch my daughter laughing and enjoying what they are doing. I watch them again the following day, when Clara teaches her how to chop and dice the vegetables, and every day after that, for two entire weeks, they tackled new recipes that made the boys produce either 'Mmmmmh yum' or a 'Yuk, what is this?' from them.

I am intrigued as I sit there watching my daughter and Clara laughing away and shake my head from side to side in disbelief, because I have never quite understood the joy people find in cooking, but it is clear watching my daughter and my half-life chirp and chop away that clearly, they too are those kinds of people. I watch this scene play out before me and witness the years I have seemingly lost.

I never quite managed to achieve a balanced family-work relationship that other working mothers have managed. I used to comfort myself with positive affirmations and rid myself of the guilt I felt when I left my babies with their father. Adam was always the better parent, but is there really such a thing? There must be because I well and truly hate to cook and pride myself in helping to make delivery apps a huge success worldwide.

Today, my daughter is making soup from fresh ingredients, which is something I never imagined she could do, partly because I couldn't do it myself. Perhaps it was merely due to my lack of interest in such elaborate cooking, but where have I been that I wasn't part of this process in her life's journey? Where did the time go; how did this happen? Having watched the movie countless times, not once did I imagine that I would one day be the co-star, producer, director, and possibly the tea lady making all the chai latte in my own show. Digging deeper into my old self is no longer the sole requirement needed to fix myself, as there seems to be a loss far greater than mine. It is the loss of time. The accident is indeed a tragedy in itself, but if I go back to the lemony stuff again, I could see how this immobile moment in my wheelchair could be my saving grace that just might allow me to be my daughter's mother once more. I feel a glow of happiness watching these two.

Clara's concern for my welfare is written all over her face. She tries hard to keep her smile, but when she thinks I am not looking, I steal a peak and notice how hard she is trying to maintain a semblance of normality in our upside-down world.

'What about the cooking, the cleaning? We need to get on top of things!' Clara says as she continues to fuss like an affectionate aunt, and I know she means well – as always. My unkempt surroundings are a clear indication of my mental space and Clara, half-life that she is, knows this only too well.

*

We're back in Zambia, and I have gone as far back as my Copperbelt University days with its grey concrete residential blocks. We have just received our government bursary meal allowance, after skipping class to be first in line, and take our long-awaited monthly trip into town to spoil ourselves on an exorbitant meal and imported biscuits that will ultimately result in us eating cereal for breakfast, lunch, and supper for the next week or so, but oh those Nutty Krusts and Bakers Eet-Sum-Mor biscuits were just so worth it.

If we had known what the future had in store for us, we might have splurged on different items. For later in life, all grown up, each and every board meeting, every workshop we attended, serves the exact same biscuits.

My half-life looks at me as we head out to lunch. I am wearing the same T-shirt I have worn for the fourth time this week. It has the words 'Team Beach' printed across it and I love it despite it being oversize, ill-fitting and totally unattractive; but still, it is my Sunday best. I wash it on Monday nights to dry on Tuesday so I that I can wear it on Wednesday. Then I wash it the very Wednesday night to dry on Thursday to be ready for Friday. A lovely routine that works perfectly well for me especially since it never gets stolen as per the many horrific stories of rampant theft of students' clothes that occur during lessons. After classes it became normal to hear someone cry out in distress the words '*Aaaahhhh ba ni bela*' repeatedly, alerting all within earshot, that the laundry thief had struck once more. It was clear to me that the laundry thief had no sense of style, for surely if they had, would not Team Beach have disappeared as well? I take one last look at myself through some half piece of mirror, and ensure I pull out the naked wires of the heating element that I had previously used to take the chill out of the cold bucket of bath water. Something all students did as the hostels had no running hot water. To this day, I have never understood why the university student hostels had hot and cold water taps when both produced cold water.

'No, Mwangala. I've had enough of 'Team Beach'. Please, take it off now and throw it away,' Clara beseeches me. I know she means well, and I cannot help questioning her and much to my amusement my puzzled response seems to irritate her further. But how can I give it up when I feel that I ought to cling on to it against all reason? Clara's frustration is palpable and although I would prefer to protest further, the trip downtown for our monthly treat far outweighs the desire to win this argument.

Years later, we would have the same 'Team Beach' sessions at my house, where Clara would come to purge my closet free from all the T-shirts with inscriptions such as *World Aids Day*, *Women's Day* or whatever annual day and company name that gave out T-shirts in size Triple XL. Surely, should not 'Team Beach' T-shirts have awards of their own for being versatile?

For instance, they can be worn as aprons in the kitchen over the actual T-shirt you intend to wear on your next outing, or as overalls whilst doing the gardening, but my all-time favourite is… (drumroll) being able to wear them as a nightshirt, finally, from Monday to Sunday without a care or the need for that mid-week wash because, being grown up, attending all those workshops, you get to collect more than a diary or a calendar at the end of the year.

Lying in bed all day means that 'Team Beach' mode is fully activated, but Clara is having none of it and I sense her disapproval. She encourages me to maintain a positive outlook in life by believing in myself and urges me to draw from my inner capabilities and strength. She suggests small steps and, needless to say, the first step on her list of capabilities is outward cleanliness.

If I want to win this mental battle, then looking dapper might help, she insists. Darn it! This appearance thing is far too much work. I argue that I maintain cleanliness – admittedly not very fashionable – but I have often felt that being both clean and fashionable require too much time and effort. Secretly, I am in awe of all the women that manage to leave their homes looking flawless, and secretly wish that I too could look like them. The good skin, the flowing Brazilian hair, glossy lips and the high-heeled shoes that seemingly make them float as they walk along so effortlessly. Alas, I am in awe of them, but only for a moment, as I quickly settle for the same 'Team Beach' look, having left a heap of clothes on the bedroom floor. It always started with a lovely pair of trousers, then numerous blouses that don't quite match, then a 'Wow, I love this blouse' moment, then numerous bottoms – still not working – then a dress, yes, a dress should do it, and then practise a sit-down to make sure it's not too tight, or examine how much of my legs will show. I curse as I go back to Team Beach because by now I'll be late for my appointment. I reach out for my 'cannot live without' product, my Vaseline, and flatten my hair edges, a quick dab on my lips and plenty more on my cracked dry elbows and run out shouting an apology to *Ba* Diana, our domestic helper, as I make a mental note to increase her salary. But my darling half-life is not like that; she is the persona of effortless flawlessness.

Get up, Mwangala, even if it is not easy, and especially when it is not easy. Make today count.

I will myself to think positively and to move, but nothing happens. The sound of Clara's voice snaps me back to reality. Clara's words are so wise and, of course, correct, but, much as I would like to, I find it difficult to respond positively. I hate to upset her like this, but all I manage to whisper are the words, 'Not today Clara, please, just not today,' and cocoon myself by wrapping my blankets tightly around my body.

The friend who can be silent with us in a moment of despair or confusion, who can stay with us in an hour of grief and bereavement, who can tolerate not knowing, not curing, not healing and face with us the reality of our powerlessness, that is a friend who cares.'

Henri Nouwen

CHAPTER THIRTEEN

ONE DAY AT A TIME

Life is easier if you tread one day at a time

Charles Schultz

My prosthesis, which is closely matched to the colour of my skin, is delivered to our home via courier in a nondescript plastic bag. It's bittersweet, because whilst I am relieved that I finally have it, not being able to wear it saddens me. I cannot use it because the doctors have insisted my reconstructed leg requires total rest if it is to heal completely. So, the irony is, what was the bad leg is now the good one. The universe definitely has a twisted sense of humour.

Finally discharged, there is the excitement of being back home after a long hospital stay. In fact, after any hospital stay, long or short, being home is simply that. It means being reunited with all your creature comforts. But alas, it is only the beginning of a gruesome journey which will test the resilience, patience and resolve of everyone in your attendance. I was not well prepared for the emotional upheaval I would go through during that process, as everything that was once familiar had to be relearnt, especially for someone missing a limb. The narrow toilet downstairs that once seemed ordinary suddenly become one of the greatest challenges I had to conquer. My wheelchair could not squeeze through the doors so it was left to the commode to be the superhero of my life.

Slowly, the strain all this is putting on my family is felt, as they escape from the strain of caring for me day and night: Adam's heavy breathing is an indicator of the stress resulting from the frequent lifting and bending over me, as he vies for position of head nurse; Nina has since given up on the award and has run off to get some air; AJ, probably the most practical of all, has demanded that I stop weeing as much as I do, and Christopher, well, Christopher is the face I hardly see and it's barely two weeks into home care. Sadly, I have to contend with everyone's misgivings. How I wish there was a catheter with a tube long enough to be casually linked to the house toilet. That wouldn't be a bad idea if it weren't so impossible and unhygienic, but for now, I guess I better get my act together sooner rather than later because this is taking a toll on my family. They need me just as much as I need them. It is all so surreal, but the sadness is real and present, and there is no way of ignoring it.

My healing has taken longer than either my family or I had expected, but the doctors knew there was no quick remedy to this. Whether I liked it or not, I have to go through the process. Unfortunately, one is never prepared enough for this kind of process. It is easy to assume it can be done especially when you have a gallery that constantly cheers you on from the bleachers but doesn't play on the field. The doctors try as humanely as is possible for them to prepare me for how some days will be so bad that I will not have the energy to think, let alone feel any kind of joyful emotion that can bring me out of my rut. It is emotionally draining on both the cared for and the caregivers.

Each one of my family members needs special care and attention inasmuch as I need to be cared for. My family needs me before we all fall apart. We are in this together, and the sacrifices they have had to make are unparalleled. In their weaknesses, they have to show strength and remain positive for me, and yet the strain on them is understated because the focus is usually on me, the person who seemingly is in a helpless position and needs more care than most. The toll on their lives is largely going unnoticed most times, but it doesn't elude me. I can see and feel what my family is going through and I can't handle it.

Adam's heavy breathing is only a symptom of what he is really going through physically and emotionally, yet he has to stand firm not only for me but for the children as well. The children as well don't know what to do, how to relate with the new mummy that isn't running around the house making sure everything is in order, and everyone's needs are met. I am the one now watching them run around, but the effects are wearing them all down. I need to get better for my family to heal; they need me. They all need psychological healing as much as I did. The accident has affected us all in different ways, and how each one of us is affected is not any less than my own trauma.

My body being shaken like a rag doll meant my immune system had also taken a nosedive. Avoiding pneumonia and other secondary illnesses has become a constant worry, and Adam, who loves to go pottering all the time, is carrying the heaviest load. After a month and two weeks of being home, he has become restless and short-tempered. I realise he needs to go out pottering as he usually does and commune with nature, and I assure him I'll be okay. He needs to go out and get some air as much as I need time alone without worrying about seeing him running around the house trying to make everything work. He makes lunch and supper in advance, a flask of tea and off he goes. The kids are in school and I'm in bed looking at the cold platter next to me. Its presence gets to me – a platter that sends a wave of nostalgia for Zambia. I think of *Ba* Diana, our housekeeper, who has become part of our family, and I make a mental note to give her a big hug the day I manage to travel back home.

Back home in Zambia, we have the blessing of having hired help, who often become a natural extension of the family. Their availability is in no way a sign of excessive living, but a matter of existence. It is job creation in a sense, but much more than that, it is an extension of parental care that working parents, especially mothers, cannot do without. Therefore, having the help at home is a need I cannot do without because my work would take me to far-off places in most instances. Aside from their father's presence, having three children all under sixteen not only needs extra help, but ensures one's sanity remains intact. On the other hand, life in the UK is very nuclear, and extra help is often unaffordable, which leaves Adam needing constant help as a carer. The level of exhaustion in him makes me feel very emotionally drained knowing there is little or nothing I can do right now to ease his burden. They all are tired and I can't pretend that they're not, although saying it out loud would only extend my guilt to them. Whether it is a case of age or the ability to speak his mind, AJ is the only one that tells me how he feels.

'Mummy, can I tell you something?'

'Yes.'

'I'm kind of glad you had the accident,' he tells me.

I hold onto my surprise and hurt, and wonder why he would say that and I ask him in a rather curious way; 'How come?'

'The teacher no longer gives me homework because I'm supposed to help you at home, but please don't tell her I don't help as much because she'll give me homework again,' he simply says.

I don't know whether to laugh or cry, but I can feel the innocence in what he is saying and I give him a big reassuring hug.

'Well, in that case, can I have a cup of tea now?'

'Aww! Mooommm! Why can't you ask Christopher?' he wails.

Some things will never change I suppose and we laugh it off.

Different friends come and go, but one of them leaves a mark. Womba and her children come to visit – another incredibly good friend, and her visit is something I need to pick me up and re-evaluate what I need for myself and my family. We have a good laugh about everything like it was before. The only thing amiss in the whole setting is that I am in bed the entire visit and not sitting at a kitchen counter making tea and laughing as we used to – the place where she and I were most comfortable. Lunch is served and all the kids take off to find their places at the table. I sit here wishing I can join them, but I wait for Nina or Adam to bring my food as per usual. Instead, Womba walks in with both her serving and mine and sits next to me as she casually talks about the chicken wings. I know that she totally gets it, and she's got me: that she was a friend – my friend. We don't say anything for a moment, and then a few seconds later, we carry on about how spicy the chicken wings are. I am choking up with emotion, but I am relieved at the same time because someone understands how I am feeling.

Situations in the healing process do have a way of lighting up a gloomy day or dragging someone deep into a ravine they can't easily come out of. I am feeling rather upbeat today and I take it as a chance to use my new prosthesis that was delivered a few weeks earlier. I didn't have the heart to use it immediately it arrived, but I guess I can try it out now. I breathe in the 'new car' smell of freshly baked leather it has as I unwrap it from the plastic it is bound in. The socket feels comfortable over the sock that is covering the stump and it feels like a perfect fit. The several months of measuring and adjusting had finally paid off. It is daunting yet also a passport that will allow me to have easier movement from the confinement of my bed, however limited it may be.

I take the first few steps to try and adjust to it, and I must have walked probably ten feet. It is amazing! It's causing me to have a funny walk – a 'lift, plunk' kind of a walk – but a walk, nonetheless. This gives me the hope I have not had in a long time, and I can now finally see the beginning of the end. The boys are excited, screaming as I show them the walk, and once more, their reactions remind me of how important it is to try and live and never give up. It is the most selfless I have been in a while having been engrossed in my pain at the exclusion of all else, and being in a new space and learning how to respond to my new environment with a new perspective on life, which will require a change in my perception and the situation I'm in. Inasmuch as I hate change, I see now that it is the very essence of growth, and I want to embrace it with all the power in my arms.

I eventually graduate to using walking sticks, though it is taking much effort to balance on them to do something I have done naturally all my life from an age I cannot remember. It is something that I, like everyone else, had taken for granted as a normal part of my life – walking. I see how everything that I had and now have is not normal because normal can change overnight, and normal can be redefined. The problem I have though is, can't I stop reliving that day? Every day, I see that car in my mind's eye and I feel myself freeze; and then I hear it – the sound of the car on my body. I don't feel it, I hear my body break. It is something like nothing I have ever heard before – the sound of a breaking body. It is a sound that haunts me still, a sound that no one must ever hear in their lifetime. What I am now is not normal; it is my survival.

So, I close my eyes and pray silently: *Lord, how did this happen? How has this made me a better person? How have I found my purpose in something so meaningless? You promised never to give us more than we can carry or did you miscalculate the weight that you have given me? I fear the load on my shoulder is too heavy for me. I cannot carry it as I am being crushed beneath it. Lord, allow me to return this load because frankly, since You allowed it, it is only fair that You, Lord, carry it.* I tell myself all these things while telling them to God as well and I need clarification and understanding of my current situation. I cannot do it still; I cannot bring myself to remember or forget *that day*.

Rather than keep questioning myself and God for something I cannot easily get an answer for, I do the next best thing: I practise my walking. 'Am I not made in the image of God? Will He not carry me through it?' My thoughts are interrupted by my son when I hear…

'Don't, Mum.' It is Christopher.

'Why not?' I ask him, wondering why he would stop me from walking and regaining my independence.

'Because I don't want you to fall and then you have to go back to the hospital,' he declares.

That statement in itself speaks all the words he has feared throughout this period, and I realise, see and acknowledge with certainty that this trauma is not mine alone. I assumed it was only I who felt the pain of that day until I saw the fear of what the accident meant to everyone around me. It was 'mummy' who nearly died. Yes, I am somebody's mummy. I am somebody's wife. I am somebody's daughter and somebody's sister. I am someone's friend. How people react, and especially children, is unprecedented. People react in different ways to the same traumatic event or incident they experience. People need counselling in whichever form it comes; everyone needs it. Some people keep things hidden and they manifest in different ways. My son, too, has his own fears.

For my son Christopher, it caused fear that I would hurt myself or that he would probably lose me. For Nina, it was the responsibility of being the older sibling taking care of her father and her siblings without the guidance of her mother. For AJ, it was not having his mummy around as the worst goalkeeper ever so he can keep scoring his goals. For Adam, well… he is buckling beneath the weight of holding up the whole family. My entire family needs counselling and there is no denying it. My life has changed just as it has for everyone in my home. I can still hear the sound of the brokenness of my body, but what is also broken is my emotion. I cry, laugh and cry again in the same day. It is a rollercoaster of emotions and it is exhausting.

'Lord, give me your strength because you have thrown me the largest curve ball yet. I no longer want to embrace my situation and my misery. I no longer want to host this solo pity-party; time to stop buying the drinks. I need to take this head-on, and I have no idea where it will lead. I have no expectations. Whatever I need to do or get to help me walk again, I will do it. I want to walk, I pray.'

The ray of sunshine has come to visit me just when I need it the most. Laura has the level of madness that exceeds mine, and her dry sense of humour perfectly suits me. When I am feeling down and out, she has a way of lifting my spirits from whichever floor they may have fallen onto. She gets my prosthesis and tries it on, and her quirkiness makes me wonder whether I should laugh or cry. She takes pictures of herself caressing the limb, and I have no clue what to do with this Spanish nurse who has become my friend. She calls me her African princess. What a blessing she has been. Her disposition makes her behave as though everything is normal, and she gets on with life around me without missing a beat. It makes me realise that I need to make the hard decisions even when I don't want to. She is showing me that I have lost a limb, not my mind or my personality.

I see now that it is time for me to just get on with it and learn how to do the one thing I hate right now – getting up. It has been the most daunting task that I have willed myself countless times to do, but I choose to crawl back into bed and shut everything out, and I know that can't go on forever. I need to do it, and I need faith and courage if I'm to walk again. However, the only way I will walk again is if I get up first – literally. I have spent three months lying on my back with nowhere to look but up, and now I am deciding to live because my life is actually worth something; it is worth fighting for. Until I place value on it and determine its worth, no one will do it for me. If other people in my situation learnt how to use what I am trying to learn, then I can do it too, but more so for me, I need to do it for myself and my family. They need me.

There is no time like now for me to get actively involved in my own life and stop lying in bed 'waiting for my grave'. Life is both short and unpredictable, and the graph is definitely not a constant line. As we go through life hoping the decisions we make give us the best results, we probably sacrifice so much in the expectation of being rewarded for the good works we perform – hoping for adulations of those who watch us (or not) making what we presume is a success of ourselves. In the process, the simple pleasures of life elude us because we keep our attention focused on the bigger picture, the grand perspective of who we hope to be. I constantly took the safest routes that had fewer detours and deviations wanting to remain on the intended path I charted for myself, but did this safe route take me to my intended destination? No, it took me on a head-on course with a drunken driver. Where is the joy in it all? It is in the simple pleasures of life, the unplanned and unmonitored, seeking no reward but just simply living one day at a time.

'Life should not be a journey to the grave with the intention of arriving safely in a pretty and well-preserved body, but rather to skid in broadside in a cloud of smoke, thoroughly used up, totally worn out, and loudly proclaiming 'Wow! What a Ride!'

Hunter S. Thompson[18]

CHAPTER FOURTEEN

I AM NOT A DUCK

'Mwangala, I have cried for days over what happened to you, and it took Fr Chilinda to make me understand. He said to me that if this is what it took for God to save your life, then praise Him for that. He saved your sister's life and that was the cost – so I'm not crying anymore. I thank God for saving my sister's life; to bury you would have been too unbearable for me.'

Nyambe Mwenda

I am paddling frantically beneath my calm disposition to keep afloat. My heightened emotions are building up in me. I want to scream as loudly as I can, to all that can hear, that – I am not a duck!

I cry out to you, Lord: Come to me – quickly! Listen to my voice when I cry out to you! ... my eyes are on you, my Lord God. I take refuge in you; don't let me die!

Psalm 141:1,8

CHAPTER FIFTEEN

CAMPFIRE

'Mwangala, must they know?'

Shenda Zukas

My old junior school classmate and friend Shenda has kindly agreed to be my carer whilst the family has left for Dubai on a pre-booked holiday. It took a lot of convincing to let my husband agree to the arrangement. But I had to remind him that the children needed to dissociate the negativity they held from my trauma. They all needed a break and, after much discussion, they left. It is the first day and she enquires as to what my bathing routine is so she can make the correct preparations. I explain to her the process of my ablutions and how to fill a basin with water in the utility room, warming up the room with an air heater, and then sponging me down using face towels whilst I'm sitting on my commode.

'Wait a minute,' she says, 'you've actually been having a bath in a bowl?' She looks shocked and I don't understand why, because there is no other way of doing it, and this is how the nurses taught me in hospital. I've been doing this for several months and, despite the awkwardness of it, it works.

'Yes,' I say to her. 'This is how the carers taught me when I came home from the hospital.'

She shakes her head in disbelief and says, 'Today is the day you will have a shower *in* the shower.'

'But Shenda, I can't go up the stairs,' I protest.

I am wondering what I'm missing here because she can clearly see I can't go upstairs because that is where the only bathroom is.

I am taken back to a childhood memory when my father once used the analogy of a campfire to illustrate to me that sometimes it takes one to show the other that a simple shift from one position to another can be a breath of fresh air.

Sitting around a log fire is a common occurrence in many African villages and Zambia is no exception. This is usually where folklore is narrated and a sense of community is built. To this day, it has not changed in many places despite the technological era we live in. Funeral homes are common places where log fires are lit, and usually men sit around the fire telling stories of past and present incidents and events. Log fires, consisting of dry, withered stumps that slowly release years of energy soaked up from the sun, producing whispering hisses and the occasional pop, and depending on the type of the wood used, almost always accompanied by a thick, intoxicating smell of whispering smoke going in different directions following the course of the wind. The stars always look brighter but the smoke left a lingering unpleasant small on your clothes.

My father, a man with confidence and always demonstrating an unwavering willingness to get things done, is a great storyteller. However, getting on in years has somewhat softened his approach to life and unfortunately, my accident did not help him in any way as it added ten years to his life. As a teenager he had spoken to me sternly when I stubbornly refused to shift my mindset on what I had thought was the correct position, 'Mwangala mwanake, when you are seated around a campfire, and you see your friends constantly rubbing their eyes because of the smoke blowing in their direction, you watch this for a while until you finally pull them away and say to them, "Move from the smoke's direction and sit here as it is not blowing this way."' That story came rushing back to me as if it were just yesterday.

Shenda's normally high-pitched voice has become soft and gentle, and the pain in her voice brings me back to the present. A few moments later I understand why. She narrates how one of the most important and sympathetic actions she had undertaken for her ailing mother when she had been caring for her was to ensure she had cascades of water over her body as a therapeutic measure. Compared to sponge baths, having running water over the body is believed to be a cleansing of sorts. But after months of sponge baths, it seemed near impossible that I would once more have the blissful sensation of water fall over my body. *She definitely has her wires twisted*, I thought to myself.

'This is a staircase we are dealing with, Shenda!' I exclaimed.

She does not relent and I have lost my will to argue. Carefully, she demonstrates how I ought to tackle each step, one at a time with upwards lifts whilst in a seated position. Having been confined to the ground floor of the house for months, I convince myself that even three steps up would be a great achievement. We are getting it done, and I grow excited and more convinced as I conquer the fourth step.

The competitive person in me feels excited to have passed a milestone, however small it would seem to another. We tackle each step until we finally get to the top where we are faced with a different challenge. The thought of my bare bottom sitting on a cold shower floor makes my skin crawl and I totally refuse to enter the shower. Undeterred, Shenda's energy and infectious girly laugh is back as she disappears down the stairs shouting behind her back.

'It's okay, Mwangala, I have a plan,' she declares with a hearty laugh. I can't help shaking my head from side to side as I wonder if it would have been easier to go to Dubai instead. Moments later, a smiling Shenda appears with an aerobic step in her hands.

'I found this in the garage, Mwangala. See. You can sit on it like this,' she says as she demonstrates.

I don't want to hurt her feelings by declaring I actually did not need that particular demonstration but I am no longer surprised or offended, as that feeling disappeared whilst I had been admitted in hospital. To this day, it baffles me as to why people assume you've lost your mind when you're an invalid or an amputee, because, whilst in hospital the nurses would come to my room and ask me in a very animated way, if I had had a poo that day.

'Good morning, my lovely,' they would say with a heavy English accent, smiling broadly. 'Have we had a *poooooo* today?' with great emphasis on the word.

A slight nod of my head in embarrassment and as if that was not enough, it was followed by a great, 'Well done, my lovely. What are we eating today?' as the same menu card that I have now memorised is placed before me.

Somebody, please, kill me now.

Shenda is invoking a lot of memories today and I fight to remain focused. I drag myself inside the shower stall and sit on the step. It is a strange but liberating feeling after so many months of confinement. I look at her wondering how she got me up and finally in here, and my heart is filled with love and gratefulness for this fairy-like person that is my friend.

Shortly after, warm water falls freely onto me and, this once, I do not mind that my hair is getting wet and the water has found its way into my eyes and nostrils, and a beaming Shenda shouts and is jumping up and down with joy.

'See, Mwangala, we did it! Call me when you're done,' and before I can turn to say thank you, she is gone. We both need this private moment for I hear muffled sobs behind the door but I am cognisant of the fact that I too could have invoked a sorrowful memory for her. I am left alone to my own sobs. But soon realise it is the first happy tear I am shedding.

Lord, thank you for Shenda, who has managed to position me away from the direction of the choking smoke.

Much later, we're at the mall, then the cinema, then Wagamama, and finally we have an easy stroll window-shopping as Shenda pushes my wheelchair in and out of the stores. I can't help but ask her repeatedly if my prosthetic leg looks like my real leg.

'Yes, it does, no one will know,' she assures me.

I ask for the umpteenth time: 'Shenda, does it look like my real leg?' I insist because my insecurity is surfacing.

This time she says, 'Yes, your legs look the same. People will think you are just paralysed,' and we both laugh at her dry joke.

I don't know whether I am relieved, but it works. I don't seem to mind much anymore. My friend thinks everything is okay. She has been amazing and we made it and that is enough. So tonight, I will be upstairs sleeping in my king-size bed rolling from side to side, and I am happy – incredibly happy.

There seems to be so much space, especially after being in a hospital bed for the last few months, and no snoring Adam that I have to kick (excuse the pun). I am rolling and laughing and rolling and laughing some more – the small things I once took for granted. I remind myself never to chastise AJ and Christopher when they jump up and down on the bed when they come back home from Dubai because I want them to scream and enjoy the simple pleasures of life.

It's the last week before she must return to Zambia and she pushes me a little further.

'Why not try two steps, because your prosthetic leg is just lying there?' Shenda says.

I'm so afraid to even try, but I rely on my physiotherapist's expertise when she said I should trust that the leg will carry me. It is not an easy thing to do, but today, I will try no matter how difficult it may seem. After all, the worst that can happen is I could fall, break something else, go back to hospital, and what's the big deal with that? I smile to myself and I begin with my first steps. One step – two steps – and at four steps, Shenda and I are screaming that I did not fall. I will not need to go to the hospital after all. I have done it without breaking anything or crying. She hugs me, almost crying again and when she lets go, I am not sure what this feeling is that l have, because I do not recognise it, as it has been so long since I last felt joy.

'Now I know I have seen the glory that cannot be unseen; I am changed as I look upon the Lord and pray'

'River Wild' by Hillsong[19]

CHAPTER SIXTEEN

NINA

'I am told many children block out the memory of trauma. In fact, the healing process can only truly begin when we are willing to remember.'

Phoebe Stone[20]

She moves around me but not with me. At the hospital, she says nothing. She moves as close to the wall as she possibly can and says nothing. I don't know how to reach out to her without feeling I am trying too much or seem like I am minimising what she's feeling with my words. I am hurting and I don't know how to deal with what my daughter is feeling or going through. She sits silently by my bedside holding my hand and once in a while I squeeze her hand in a reassuring manner.

Christmas morning brings out the excitement in the boys. We take pictures together; she's smiling as she and her brothers take turns to be by my bedside, all the while being careful not to expose the 'no leg'. She's laughing and talking endlessly about everything and nothing, and is careful not to talk about 'that'.

Finally discharged from hospital and having settled as best as I can at home, she helps me to bathe and dress up, and helps me in and out of my wheelchair, and she is still politely quiet. She doesn't say much even when we're alone, and does everything almost mechanically, the way she was shown by the nurses, and once in a while offers me a warm smile. I don't know what to say to her although there is so much that is pent up within me that I want to burst from feeling my daughter's pain, but I am helpless.

During my session with the psychologist, I was encouraged to share my emotions with the children and the effects the accident had on me and the household. Thinking I knew better being their parent, I say nothing to Nina but make continuous observations of every move she makes. After all, it is my firm belief that observation is crucial before making any assessments, but her silence and quiet disposition is unsettling and I want very much to reach out to my daughter and comfort her. I know she's hurting, but I'm not sure what I should do to get her to open up and tell me what she's feeling. She has created a barrier around herself that I can't penetrate. I need to try, however hard it will be, as am certain she needs me as much as I need her. *Lord, help me to get through to my daughter.*

The front door opens unexpectedly and Nina walks through from school. She finds me on the floor shuffling on my bottom towards the bedroom upstairs. It has been such a major transition for me coming from being permanently confined downstairs in the converted living room space to having the choice of moving around the house on my own. It was daunting at first but has become more liberating now. Seeing me on the floor startles her but she quickly composes herself and with a 'Hi Mom, I'm back,' disappears into her room. I sit there for a bit wondering what I should do next and am somewhat embarrassed and guilty about being found like that. I call out to her and ask her to help me off the floor onto my bed, which she obligingly performs in effortless swoop. *Praise God for gymnastic classes.*

'Thank you,' I say as I let out a nervous laugh.

'Sure, whatever,' comes out from her expressionless face. She doesn't seem connected to what she has done or how she feels about it. I am hoping the laugh and the smile would break the imaginary wall she has erected but that doesn't do much for her either. My face feels frozen with this grin that I can't brush off quickly enough without seeming disappointed. I bury my face in the pillow and let out a silent scream to release the frustration I feel for not being strong enough for my children. I couldn't bear the sight of my daughter seeing me on the floor. I am breaking inside, but I have to show Nina that it is okay with me even though it isn't for both the comfortable and uncomfortable situations. Everything can't be perfect and everything can't be a mess. There has to be a middle ground. But what was it exactly?

After the shower incident with Shenda, my shuffling skills had improved considerably. Seeing as I can't kneel, crawling, which might be a faster way of moving around, is out of the question at this point. Therefore, shuffling on my bottom is the best I can do under the circumstances, and it works for me. Perhaps I should have prepared my children more as the sight of me on the floor may have been disturbing to them, who had always considered me, like all other children with their parents, to be an invincible hero. This is a first for all of us but it is something that I need to acccpt, acknowledge, and embrace as my new way of doing things. I only hope my daughter will see that there is nothing else that can be done at this stage other than accepting that my physiology has been changed forever. But how will I help her find closure?

Enjoying my new-found freedom, I decide to head to the kitchen for no apparent reason, and as I shuffle toward the landing to the stairs, Nina opens her bedroom door, wanting to go the same direction but upon seeing me on the floor, she chooses to close her door and retreat to her room. *Great.*

I had hoped the sessions with the shrink would have enabled her to be more open about her feelings, but her quiet demeanour meant she preferred to cry herself to sleep on most nights, especially having found herself in an unwarranted role of mother over her siblings. She is their elder sister, but she is still my little girl that has taken a parental role because she can see I need help. I battle with these emotions because I know how unfair all this is to her, and I have nothing but admiration for her, now more than ever. If there ever was a reason for me to get better, this was it.

So, it was on that early morning at 2am that Nina covered her eyes with the sleeve of her oversized jumper and let out a gut-wrenching sob, which tore my heart to shreds. I was hurting inside and I wanted to cry with her, but instead I waited it out. After she regained some sort of composure, she blurted it out.

'You are the one that looks after us. It is you who is the most active in the house. The boys are out of control. Dad lets them have their way, so I have to shout at them all the time. You sit in bed and sit on the floor all the time. It is not you, Mom.' She paused for a moment. 'Then there is this girl at school who's so mean to me. Today, I sat and had lunch on my own, but she's so mean… I want my mom back…' then sobbed some more.

I calmly said all the right things she needed to hear about life to calm her grieving soul, but I knew what she needed the most was her mother – me. Lying there in my living room while the rest of my family slept upstairs, I cried out to God – angry and thankful to be alive, if only to live for that moment to hold my sixteen-year-old daughter in my arms and rock her back and forth like I used to when she was a baby, and reassure her with my words in a whisper: 'Nina, I'm still here.'

Nothing else would have made her feel better than having her mother back. I was still her mommy and there was nothing to add or subtract from it. I wiped her tears and she cracked some random bad joke that made us both laugh. As she went back upstairs and I was left alone in what had become familiar darkness, I fully understood and appreciated how much my daughter needed me.

I glared at the bottle of morphine perched on the nightstand like an enemy and decided enough was enough and proceeded to empty its contents into my commode, then curled up into a foetal ball and cried – all the time reassuring myself, 'Mwangala, you're still here. Lord, I'm still here.' I needed to live if not for myself at least for my children, and slowly I began to have more reasons to live than to die.

'Every man's life ends the same way. It is only the details of how he lived and how he died that distinguish one man from another.'

Ernest Hemingway[21]

CHAPTER SEVENTEEN

CHRISTOPHER

'Then again, he supposed the healing process in contrast to trauma was gentle and slow... the soft closing of a door, rather than a slam.'

J. R. Ward[22]

He has found me crying and he stands there silently watching me. I look at him and I'm struggling to stop the tears from running down my face, attempting to falsify strength but I'm failing. The sight of him makes me weak; I can't deal with this. My son is hurting. How can I make it easier on him? How can I stop my children from being a part of all this mayhem that is going on around us? I can't handle it. I am breaking apart, but my children need me. They need their mother back in whichever form she may be. Surely, my son should not witness his mother's breakdown at such a tender age. Am I not, as Nina says, the pillar of strength of this family? Am I not the formidable Mwangala that doesn't buckle down no matter the enormity of the challenge? All I can do now to manage the situation is to whisper: 'Christopher, Mummy is okay. Please go upstairs and play.'

He doesn't move. His lower lip slowly breaks into a tremble, and the harder I try to hide my tears, the stronger the sobs become and I can't stop this torrent of tears in front of my son. After what seems like a lifetime and the dark cloud that has overshadowed me begins to lift, I manage to compose myself and I look up. He is still standing there. My helpless arms beckon him and I pull him toward me in a bear hug that crushes the frame of my skinny boy into my cuddle and I whisper in his ear, 'I'm okay, Mummy loves you.'

He reciprocates and gives me a big squeeze and he lets me go. Silently, he walks out of the room and says nothing. I am crushed and I know there is so much brewing under all that trembling because everything isn't making sense to my boy. His perspective of our life as he knew it has suddenly been upturned into a horror movie he doesn't want to watch. The joy he felt and the simple pleasures of laughter have disappeared in our home and there is nothing he can do about it. I could feel in his hug that he wants everything to be back the way it used to be, but it can't. Things have changed; I have changed; we have changed. How much have we changed? I don't know, but one thing I know for sure is that whatever state I am in, I want my family to feel joy again. I want my darling Christopher to feel the joy of being a child again.

The day goes by with little incident, but that encounter keeps replaying itself in my head. It's been put on a loop that keeps replaying itself. I keep seeing my broken son in my moment of weakness and the guilt that I can't shake off leaves me tossing and turning all night. Daybreak, and my sleep-deprived eyes are woken by the gentle tugs at my shoulder.

'Wake up, Mummy,' he says.

'I'm awake, I'm awake, what is it, Christopher?' I ask with heavy eyelids, wondering what the urgency is.

'Mummy,' he says, 'if you had won the election, would you have gone to hospital still?'

Oh Lord, how innocent yet so profound. I have an inkling of where this might be going although I didn't expect that the question would ever come up; in some way, it doesn't seem strange that he has asked.

'Yes, Christopher, I would have,' I say, trying not to quizzically look at him.

'No, Mom, I don't think so because I was thinking, if you had won the election, you would have got the job to be an MP, and you wouldn't have been riding your bike, and you wouldn't have fallen down and ended up in hospital, and you wouldn't have been crying last night,' he rumbles on, trying to fit all the scenarios in a single sentence short of running out of breath.

Momentarily, I'm at a loss for words, but I look at him trying hard to hide my worry through my bloodshot eyes, for that must have been too much torment for someone at such a tender age of eleven.

'No, Christopher, I would still have been involved in an accident, still would have gone to the hospital and would have still been crying because even if I had won the election, I would still have gone riding that day. Christopher, accidents happen. Yesterday you found me crying because I was having a bad day, but today, I'm going to have a good day.'

I say it to him calmly though I am shaking inside, and I try to explain to him further that, in life, bad things always happen just as good things happen as well, but as long as the good outweighs the bad, we will be okay. I realise he is not convinced but is also clever enough to know when to let it go for today. There and then, I am reminded of how easy it is to talk about good and bad, and being strong, and yet I was failing to implement what I know and believe in. I am not even sure whether I am now a victim or a conqueror, but I need to be a conqueror for the sake of my children. I know that my son is silently watching and observing me, and clearly does not share as much as I hoped he would.

My greatest fear is not necessarily about being strong in my son's presence. My greatest fear is about making every moment the ledge on which he can stand and see further than what is currently in front of him. That is much more than reassuring him everything is and will be okay. It is about helping him to assert himself and understanding that bad things happen even to good people. I don't want it to become something that will have him ending up on the *XYZ Show* explaining to the world how this one moment messed him up for life, but should rather be that it built him into becoming an assertive man in his adulthood.

'Gracious Lord, please give me strength.'

'There is a crack in everything,
That's how the light gets in.'

Leonard Cohen[23]

CHAPTER EIGHTEEN

AJ

'Tears shed for another person are not a sign of weakness; they are a sign of a pure heart.'

José N. Harris[24]

'Mommy, have you been in bed all day?' he asks me.

I gently nod my head and tears begin to swell in his eyes and I realise in that moment that it is time for me to put on my mask and be brave for my son.

'Mommy, you used to be fun because you used to play football with me and do fun things like take me to Marks & Spencer for the snake-shaped sweets, but you don't do any of that. Is it because of your leg?' he asks as tears spilled over the sides of his eyes.

I pull him towards me and my voice cracks as I say to him, 'AJ my baby,' and I notice he does not protest when I call him baby as he usually did, 'I will play football with you again, and I definitely will take you to buy those sweets you love, and we will do all the fun things we used to do together again.'

'But when, Mommy?'

'Soon, AJ, soon. I just need to learn how to walk again. Meanwhile, please go and ask Daddy to bring me some tea, and can you go and brush your teeth?'

'Okay, Mom,' he says, and grudgingly frees himself from my tight embrace.

I can't cry, not now, though I have a pain in my chest that makes me reach out to clutch it trying to stop the onset of the pain wave. It cannot be a heart attack because my left arm is not tingly, and it cannot be a stroke because my face is not twisted, but that's what it feels like as I attempt to self-diagnose. This pain will not go away however hard I try to rationalise it. But soon it dawns on me that the pain I feel is from my broken heart.

Three weeks later, I am motionless as AJ comes bursting in with a story about this and the other and runs out again. It crosses my mind that the thought of my children seeing me like this day after day when life has been given to me will only make them disbelieve all the 'power' talks I used to give them at breakfast before the school runs. I constantly preached to them on the differences between a cat and a pig. Both would fall into the mud and whilst one would immediately get up and lick itself clean, the other would lie there wallowing and enjoying the slippery mud. I have now turned into that pig – lying here wallowing in my own sorrow and buying the drinks to my own pity-party.

'Get up, Mwangala, your children still need you.'

I put on my prosthesis and prepare to do physio and a tear trickles down my face from the discomfort and pain it causes me. It seems what was a perfect fit has now become unfit and needs further adjustment. However, I am standing and that's all that matters. I decide now that each time I cry, it will be whilst I'm standing and not whilst am lying down. I'll cry all the way to Marks & Spencer and buy AJ the snake-shaped rubbery disgusting sweets that he loves so much if I must. AJ, my darling AJ. The thought of your bubbly personality gave me a fighting chance to live. Why then am I lying here dying? Why then should I lie here dying from grief?

Oh, how painful sadness is. This is my ultimate failure and betrayal of self; to survive a trauma such as I did only to die of a broken heart. It is believed that when it's hardest to hold on, then hold on the hardest. I understand it now and I cry out to my God to show me His face because my hands are raw from holding onto Him so tightly. My children are the reason I am alive today yet here I am denying them the pleasure of my presence. They see me, but they don't have me.

Get up, Mwangala, you need to be AJ's mummy again.

'When you're at the end of your rope, tie a knot and hold on.'

Theodore Roosevelt[25]

CHAPTER NINETEEN

TRANSFORMER

Trauma is personal. It does not disappear if it is not validated. When it is ignored or invalidated, the silent screams continue internally heard only by the one held captive. When someone enters the pain and hears the screams, healing can begin.'

Danielle Bernock[26]

I am of the opinion that the different views and perspectives we have about life are wide and varied; the word tolerance comes to mind. One person's view is not a reflection of the collective opinion. How we handle trauma and its offshoots is not a standard template that should apply to all. We are individuals, and therefore, have unique ways of dealing with our situations and are not subject to the standards that people apply for us.

I am in physio and we are having a conversation, or rather what I would call a debate, on why I'm wearing a prosthesis that has the appearance of my real leg. This is a choice I consciously made to have my prosthesis to be as close to my skin tone as possible.

'Why not leave it exposed to show the metal components of the prosthesis?' they ask, querying me on my choice of prosthesis since they seem to have pride and acceptance in what they opted to wear.

'It is because I want my life back to as normal as it possibly can be, which involves having my prosthesis having the likeness of my other leg,' I say, totally infuriated that I should be questioned about my preference.

Physio has become a daily routine where I have begun to make friends with people I have found and new ones who joined us at a later stage. All the guys say they love their exposed metal parts that form their prosthesis because it embraces the change they have gone through, and that their prostheses make them look like the popular 'Transformer' figures. They chatter away about how they are not afraid to show the world how their lives have been transformed, and frankly, how cool it simply looks. They argue that to cover the leg is a form of embarrassment or failure to accept that I have lost a limb. Quickly I realise that I'm outnumbered as I am the only female for 'the covering' team against the eight gentlemen against the 'the exposed' team.

This is no longer a debate but a school yard brawl, and one that I will not engage in. I'm exhausted and saddened by their viewpoint. Why can they not see the pain this debate-turned-fight is causing me, but how can they? They are not me, and I am not them. I choose to spend my time these days arguing less; there is no point really. People are entitled to their own opinions. I used to be a person that needed to make people understand my viewpoint. I will be quick to admit that perhaps a pinch of arrogance was in the formula. In reality, when you come close to death as I did, your values change as do your priorities. The greatest thing is I have stopped being so self-centred and I 'see' others more. I have 'empathy' – an emotion my sister Linda swears I never developed until now; Sod's Law I suppose. I decide to wheel myself away from this debate and feel pleased with my new wheelchair skills, which help me navigate myself to any place I choose, and right now, 'any place' is not here.

Tolerance is what I am learning – acceptance of other people's viewpoints and embracing my own feelings and views. It is okay to have other people disagree with me. Once upon a time, I would have stayed to fight my viewpoint and shove my opinion down their throats to disable their voices from ever being heard. But that was the old obstinate me that nearly died. Just as I am learning to be more tolerant, I hope that the 'against' team can also understand my desire for that particular type of prosthesis. I accept varied viewpoints, but again, I don't have to accept them if they are contrary to what I want for myself. Hence, I have found it easier and more liberating to merely wheel away from opposing views.

But one such opposing view I could not wheel myself away from was the sneak preview I gave myself during a break in my shrink sessions. In my file were the words:

'The patient has not come to terms with her new reality and is living in denial. She may need to be counselled further. She has a supportive family system that may also need to be counselled, especially the children.'

I mean, seriously, new reality? My foot! (Oops no pun intended.) I thought the prognosis was rather extreme despite the truth in it. As I sit on the steps at the hospital, waiting for the hospital transport to return me to my safe zone, there is a chill on my face that tells me the sun's heat is waning today, yet I look up and smile. I take a peek at my skin-tone prosthesis and compare it with my other leg and smile wistfully.

'I am not a Transformer.' I say it under my breath and I whisper toward the glittering sun that holds the promise of a new beginning.

'Transform the sun and beat the wind,' I say, and it could have been the effect of the drugs I was taking at the time, but I am sure that the sun winked at me.

'Fairy tales do not tell children the dragons exist. Children already know that dragons exist. Fairy tales tell children the dragons can be killed.'

G. K. Chesterton[27]

CHAPTER TWENTY

SHAKEN

'The process you're going through requires that you deal with yourself first before anything else. The rest, Mwangala, is simply a luxury.'

John Sangwa, SC

'If I hear one more sermon about life and light at the end of the tunnel, going through the valley or the words "it shall come to pass", I will literally throw up.' I found myself saying out loud what had been on my mind for a while during a conversation I had with Fr Simatende who relentlessly encouraged and prayed for me.

'With blessings, first is the burden. We go through pain to live to see the blessing,' he responded graciously in a pious sort of way.

I stared at him blankly and wondered whether anyone had anything to say about what exactly goes on between those unequal places of blessing and burden. The pain I feel is not transitory, with no timeline or destination. It is a constant throb that reminds me of its presence and my loss. There is no remission from it however much I try to ignore it. Has it ever occurred to anyone that the burden I carry may be too great and too heavy for me to bear, and that I may simply collapse under its weight? Has anyone understood that the pain may be unbearable for me, and that it is possible to die in that infamous tunnel, which clearly the whole world knows about but secretly hopes they never find the entrance to? I am reminded of something I read in one of the countless inspirational books I used to read, which described how a bridge is designed for transitory load and not static load.

'Lord, did You not promise me a transitory load that I could carry, and one that I could bear? Is there any possibility for me to say without sounding blasphemous that You may in fact have miscalculated my load? How many more other miscalculations are there, Lord? How many did not make it through that tunnel or that valley of death, how many Lord? I cry out to you my God, grasping for any kind of response, but all I hear is silence. Why, Lord, have you turned your face from me? Am I alive because You looked at me? Say something, Lord, say anything.'

I never once discarded the old religious rites and teachings I learnt from my younger days, which I believe I tapped into during my crash when my single cry out to the Lord was to truly save me. Before I felt the impact, I asked of the Lord not to take me because my children still needed me, and He did. Throughout my ordeal right up to surgery, I believed I was a good Christian, and naturally, I believed God would reward me for being good, and would prove to all the surgeons that I served a living God. At that time, I was spirit filled with the happy-clappy messages having read books written about how I should stay the course and keep my faith for the sole purpose of being the best version of me. Yet, I could not ignore the fact that I was disappointed when I did not receive the healing I sought, which would have prevented the surgery and saved my leg. So, writing this memoir and reliving my experience is an attempt to share about finding hope, meaning, and purpose in my journey, and to reconnect with the higher being (God) that I wanted to heal my physical being when He was already working on my inner one.

My inner voice is screaming for a sparring partner. Can someone please tell me how to make it through this tunnel? Can someone please shout out to me, 'Mwangala, the light is beautiful, and it is worth it? It will not blind you after all the darkness that surrounds you.' I need someone who is in my wheelchair to say to me, 'I hear you; I see you; I know you; and yes… try harder… the valley is but for a brief moment. Do not give up because you are almost there.'

In dealing with myself, I told John that I had got to a point where I was questioning my faith, only holding onto a string. I was questioning how all those Sunday masses at Roma Girls, all those pretty clothes that Mum made us wear to church, the communion classes, the confession in that dark wooden box where I spent more time trying to peep through the tightly woven wooden trellis of the confessional booth to see who was telling me to say ten Hail Marys for my sins and those sacraments, and how they all seem like a distant memory with no way of helping me now. 'Lord, tell me – of all the sacraments, is death your favourite? Tell me please, because I'm hanging by a thread here as I hold onto your promises. I need to hear you. Please speak to me. I am shaken.'

I see her as she lay there thinking: 'If I could only touch the hem of His garment…' I see you now, sister; I hear you now, sister; I know you now, sister. I can feel the pushing, the shoving – the scramble all over you as you wait for that moment for Him to pass by you. Her pain is now my pain, and I feel what she felt especially now when I am going through my own battle. I am wrestling to find the gap that will lead me to the hem of His garment that I may touch it and stop my own bleeding. I need to get to Him that He may see me as I am. My soul needs healing.

When questioned by Gay Byrne[28] on the Irish TV show about the meaning of life, and what he might say to God at the pearly gates of heaven, Stephen Fry – the English actor, comedian, and writer said; 'How dare you! How dare you create a world in which there is such misery that is not our fault! It is not right. It's utterly, utterly evil. Why should I respect a capricious, mean-minded god who creates a world which is so full of injustice and pain?' Then the world rose up against him saying he was blasphemous. However, it was his expression of how he perceived his world. When you're in the fray, so much makes sense and there are no logical answers that can quieten your questions. I have my own share of questions as well.

Do I feel that too? Do I blame God for what had happened to me? Do I find comfort in Him as my protector and giver of my life? My faith is absolutely challenged. So many more questions are raised within me: 'Why me, Lord, where were You? Why didn't you hear my prayer, Lord? Was I not good enough? Did I not follow Your commandments? Why choose me to be the lesson?' With time, my questions became one. 'Why do this at all, Lord?' I begged, I pleaded, I negotiated with God before the amputation, but He did not answer *my* way. I wanted a response that would suit and match *my* need. As far as I was concerned, what was so wrong in making such a request for a life-changing situation in my own way? Why not grant me that luxury? Subconsciously, the failure of my prayer for healing never once made me doubt the power of God; nonetheless, I still felt betrayed by Him.

As far as I could see then, He 'chose' not to heal me, and it became difficult for me to pray because it seemed pointless. What would I be praying for? Pray for what? My greatest fear happened and I stared death in the face, and I know I survived by His grace, but all for what – for this? I feel as though I am now living a second-tier kind of life similar to being thrown out of the king's inner court and made to be an outsider. However, what is not further from my conscious mind is, He saved me from the clutches of the devil's outstretched hand that was ready to take my life. I should have died, and when I cried out to the Lord, mercy said 'no'. Woe unto me for the devil had already touched me. My life was spared for he had no authority to take my life; it was not yet my appointed time according to God's will.

At the time of my accident, I would say I was in peak form. I was riding my ride the best way I knew how. I believe I was making a success of myself and what I set out to achieve. Despite losing the parliamentary election, I had achieved great success in every other area of my life, so that losing the coveted parliamentary seat was only losing another feather in my cap. My career was going well. I had experienced life on the campaign trail that enhanced my perception of the people I wanted to serve, and I was enjoying biking, my midlife crisis, and getting the experience I needed. I was happy. Yet, in a moment, a lifetime was gone – in just a single moment.

I did not only lose my physical independence, but I lost my emotional independence as well. Being a naturally independent person, finding myself now being taught the basics all over again is a bitter pill I am failing to swallow. Having someone help me to dress, bathe or move from one place to another has left me feeling stripped of the little dignity I thought I had left. I lie in my bed, then into my wheelchair to go to physio, and finally getting the prosthesis that should aid me to walk, albeit slowly. I used to be constantly in a hurry to get things done, and this new life I am now experiencing has caused me great frustration. Who would have thought that putting my arm through a T-shirt by myself would be considered a major milestone? Yet here I am feeling as though I have achieved something of great importance beyond my expectation.

I have grieved the loss of my leg, and no amount of prayer can make me the same person I was physically. I have mourned being labelled as a person living with a disability despite the discounted train tickets and the preferential treatment I get at the cinema. They have all failed to bring my mojo back. I cannot envision any achievements in my state with all my physical limitations reminding me of whom I cannot be and of what I cannot do. I need to dig deeper to see beyond what my eyes can see.

Tramadol and morphine took away the physical pain, but no number of painkillers can ease the pain of a broken heart. I cry endlessly and feel overwhelmed by my inner emotions. I become depressed and anxious, pushing my husband away in the process as he tries his best to take it on the chin, all the while hoping it is a passing phase. The professional help I am getting encourages me to start reliving my life and to go back to my old routines. It doesn't seem appealing, but I know I need to if I am to achieve being myself again. I have started driving lessons in an adapted car so that I can go anywhere by myself without asking Adam to drive me. I need to feel a sense of purpose and independence away from everyone else and see how I can adapt. Unfortunately, on my first solo drive, a car comes round a bend faster than I expect forcing me to close my eyes momentarily and freeze. It was hard to tell Adam what had happened because I was afraid of losing my newly acquired independence. So, for all the fear and anxieties I felt, I chose to share with my objective friend John instead.

'Mwangala, you have to first deal with yourself before anything else,' John said. He seemed to always have the right words to say even when it wasn't what I would have wanted to hear in his usual soft-spoken voice.

'Lately, talking to you is hard. I am afraid to say anything to you because you bite, but *mwana*, even I can no longer take it. You're aggressive, and inasmuch as I am trying to understand what you're going through, perhaps it is time that you take time away from all of us. You do not realise how your words hurt me sometimes. I miss our friendship and our laughter. So, take time out. You will find me when you are ready because if you carry on like this, I'm choosing to walk away from you, which will seem unfair at such a trying time as this, but it's for my own sanity,' he said.

I was shaken, and it seemed I was losing not only myself, but those around me as well. I could not simply pretend to move on because it would catch up with me later.

'Forgive whoever needs forgiving, and most of all, deal with yourself,' he added as if twisting the knife into the wound from the earlier painful words.

I took the next available flight out of the UK and went to Zambia where there would be no husband, no children, and no shrink, no one to wear my different masks for. I sat on the floor for two whole weeks crying, filled with exhaustion. I went into the garden and sat there with a glazed look; another milestone achieved. The next best thing was to watch a movie and it was then that I watched *Collateral Beauty*[29] where I heard the words:

Love, time, death
I'm trying to fix my mind.
You lost a child, Howard. It'll never be fixed.

What an *Aha* moment it was – a weight load lifted. What relief, what a joy! I felt like finally someone felt the way I did. I am not mad, insane or about to go crazy after all. Somebody else gets it. So what if it was a fictional movie? Someone real wrote those words. What I have been going through is a death of sorts, and I have been grieving the loss of my old self. I cannot be fixed based on my old specs. Not all the physio in the world, all the self-help books and audio tapes or sermons on YouTube can fix me. I lost my old self and I have to be willing to learn to be a new me. What I have been seeking in part is for someone to acknowledge my grief – to say, 'Yes, I see you and I hear you.'

A depressed actor forced me to confront who I was in my grief and not the false character I was projecting onto those I loved. Now, I want them to understand me without my having to show them how bitter and angry I am about what has happened to me, for they deserve my love and care, and most of all my sanity.

I have to find my greater purpose in life even if it is through losing a part of me that slowed me down and forced me to smell the coffee. I have to stop portraying myself in the negative and acknowledge that I do have a disability, but, and a huge but, I am still Mwangala. I have to forgive myself and to forgive the unknown man who drove his car into my body. Only then will I be able to say, *Thank you Lord for saving my life*, and mean it.

'The truth is, unless you let go, unless you forgive yourself, unless you forgive the situation, unless you realise that the situation is over, you cannot move forward.'

Steve Maraboli[30]

PART THREE
FORGIVENESS

'To be a Christian means to forgive the inexcusable because God has forgiven the inexcusable in you.'

C. S. Lewis

CHAPTER TWENTY-ONE
WHAT NEXT?

'You are fearless, Mwangala. You're one of the toughest cookies I know. You got this. (But Kaumbu, am just hanging by the ropes). That's it. The ropes are a good place to rest, to regroup. You take a few body shots on the ropes, but you keep your head down. You regroup, you refocus, and then you come out swinging.'

Kaumbu Mwondela

Fear has swayed my better judgement to let go of the ropes and has caused me to fail to move past my accident. My mortality mocking my foolish belief that I was invincible. But the time to get up has come. No one and nothing is holding me back because I know all the right things that need to be done. I have read the book, listened to the podcast, and even watched the movie, but what next? I have discovered my body has limitations which either never existed or I was indifferent to them and shattered the confidence I once had. Months of lying in my hospital bed, on the ward and at home, using a 'granny' walker to shuffle from room to room, has a way of making you feel defeated. But I wear my face with each shuffle as my boys come racing through the door shouting,

'Common, Mom. You can do it,' and immediately my last-born child breaks into the iconic James Brown dance movements.

So, what next? Kaumbu, lawyer, man of God, that one friend who listens to you intently and then at the end of a two-hour monologue, he makes one profound statement, and today is no different. Come out swinging, he says, I have had my head down for too long and it's time to come out swinging. But am struggling to grow towards rebuilding my life, that I may be present in my family's life again. The only way to stop feeling like a burden on my family is to regain my mobility and reduce the dependency I have on my care assistant. I just need to hear His voice, but still, He is far from me. *Why am I holding myself back? What am I waiting for? Kaumbu, the ropes are a comfortable and safe place for me for now. But I know I need to keep trying to get over this hurdle.*

I realise in this moment that I have created mental road maps and epitaphs of what and how I want to memorialise events in my healing process. People use different milestones to measure their progress, and I based my milestone how I thought God should answer me in order for me to find the closure I so desperately sought. Instead, God sends a message through the doctor informing me that it would take a minimum of two years for my body to fully recover from the amount of damage caused by the impact of the crash. My immediate desire is to scream, but I keep my cool. After all, I need to be rational about this. Two years is not a long time to wait on something considering the glacial movement of nature. Furthermore, the doctors need to assess during this furlough period any effects the medication I have been on could have masked. Whichever way I look at it, there is no getting out of this and I need to heal; waiting for that jail sentence to elapse while nature, nurture, and medication play their part.

I need to find a creative way to pass the time and not regard it as my wasted years. I must find purpose – purpose that will bring meaning to my life. The phone call has left my mind racing and wondering what the two-year period will mean to me and almost irritated at the curve ball in the form of another Mount Kilimanjaro to climb.

Kaumbu, I'm hanging onto the ropes and not sure how I will come out swinging when life has slowed me down intentionally for two whole years. Unable to regain my mobility at lightning speed, I stare intently at the clock, counting down as each hand moves at a snail's pace. A decision is made in the dead of night to enrol at the University of Manchester and study for an MBA programme I never had time for. More of Sod's Law for me. I hope to learn not so much to be a winner, but how not to lose. University of Manchester, here I come.

Sometimes, unplanned choices turn out to be the best choices we make. We have no power or foresight to predict the future, but as long as I live, I am prepared to meet my future and dictate the terms of my recovery to create an illusion of control that I seem to not have at all.

It is merely two years and in retrospect, I should have died, so, every day for the next two years will bring a fresh taste in my mouth. *Thank you, Lord. What a privilege. What a blessing.* This is what my 'What next?' shall be because I will not cry and spend the next two years feeling sorry for myself. I need a new lease of life. I am going to learn how to do things differently and slowly as I heal *my* way. I lost an election, and I lost a leg, but I'm still here. Every moment must count as something significant or pointless, but it shall be well lived.

As I embark upon my school journey, so do the mental games, and the manifestation of my limitations. The desire to quit weighs heavy upon me as I continue to remind myself why I started it in the first place. Knowing there would be challenges, the feeling to quit so early on in the game catches me unaware. Why am I submitting to my limitations when my mental state tells me otherwise? Shouldn't I refocus and make this moment count? Didn't I pledge to come out swinging at anything and everything so long as it was movement to help fulfil a purpose and a goal? I'm no longer afraid, and after you hit rock bottom, I have found, in a rather uplifting way, that fear is not that scary after all. Where you go or what you do next is all a construct of how you condition your mind. When things get rough and tough, God presents you with ideas, people and things that will direct the course of your journey. I dare not look in the mirror that would reveal my secret inner troubles, so instead I pray to The Almighty, to start redirecting some gifts.

'What you are is God's gift to you, what you become is your gift to God.'

Hans Urs von Balthasar[31]

CHAPTER TWENTY-TWO

NOT FULLY GROWN

'Better to live with a broken knee than to die with a good knee.'

Dr Taylor

My new-found hope, peace and independence have given me leverage to create regular routines for myself. I have gone back to reading books I love and not seeking answers to my endless questions about living and dying. I am enjoying the fresh aromas of the tea I drink, which I now I sip with such relish. I am a work in progress because there is much that I need to let go of, and I am embracing this abundance that is coming forth from my soul. The phone ringing suspends my positive thoughts and it's John on the other end.

'Hello *mwana*. Just wanted to check how you're doing.'

It's always a pleasure speaking to John calmly without the hysterics of how messed up my life has been.

'*Maweee*,' I yell in fear.

'Mwangala, what is it? Hello, hello?'

Something is moving across my arm – there it is – a green creature. I throw the book I had in my hand as well as the phone. Everything I try to flick it off with isn't working. I keep missing it more out of fear than its insistence to hang on. It moves further up toward my shoulder and I scream even louder as I try to run. My instinctive reaction is to step on the floor and keep a distance from this menace, but I land on the floor with a heavy thud. Now my scream is even louder than before when I realise what has just happened – an amputee's greatest fear.

For the first time in over a year, I had fallen to the ground. Falling poses a grave danger because the lack of balance can easily send one into objects and obstacles that cannot be avoided. With both arms and legs, someone can instinctively reach out to break the fall or use a foot to stop the motion. I don't have that luxury any more, which had been a natural reflex until now. What the mind knows and registers does not correspond with the body's reaction. The pseudo leg I feel, which my mind tells me exists, is my phantom limb.

The phantom limb deceives the mind into thinking the amputated limb is still there. It is accompanied with pain of varying degrees. The limb is present in its non-presence, and having had two legs all my life, my brain is still conditioned to walking with two legs and naturally, it follows that I would want to step with both feet. But as I jump off the bed to 'run', I instinctively step on the ground with the 'leg' that is only present in my head. A heavy thud and I crash-land.

I get hysterical in view of the gravity of my fall as my stump has not fully healed. I carry on screaming and crawling away from the creature, and I can still hear John's voice on the phone across the room shouting to find out what had happened.

Nina comes running up the stairs, pushes the door open and after a quick assessment, she walks over to me and in a soft comforting voice she says, 'It's okay, Mom, I'll get you up,' and in one strong movement, she slips her arms beneath mine and lifts me back onto the bed. She repeatedly says, 'It's okay, Mom, I've got you… it's okay, Mom, you're okay.' Her gentleness and calmness in light of the situation moves me enough to stop the high-pitched noises I am making. She then gently scoops the green creature into her cupped hands and throws it out the window.

'What was that?' I ask her, visibly shaken and wondering what the creature was.

'It was a grasshopper, Mom,' she says, and I see the concern on her face that is rather unusual. The thought of a grasshopper on my arm gives me the creeps, but I think to myself that I may have overreacted to its presence. But how I wished I had given it a befitting end, considering all the distress it has caused me, but Nina saved it. All her life, Nina has been gentle with God's creatures, and the green creature was another one she had managed to save.

She jumps onto the bed and lies next to me looking pensive. I am now worried that she may be more traumatised than I think, especially after finding me on the floor and 'saving me'.

'What's on your mind? Are you okay? I'm so sorry for screaming,' I ask.

'It wasn't fully grown; I wonder if it made the fall,' she says in a contemplative manner.

'What fall?' I ask her now, confused about what she's talking about.

'The grasshopper, Mom, it wasn't fully grown. I'm upset that I threw it out the second-floor window. It may not have made the fall.' Her voice sounded numb from worry.

My insides scream with joy. Finally, it is not about me. Her worry and focus is on something else and a wave of relief passes over me. It is no longer about me. My Nina is back.

'Hello, hello, John,' but the line is thankfully dead.

A few weeks later during one of my regular doctor's visits, Dr Taylor sees the anxiety on my face and asks me what I was afraid of as my recovery process was on track.

'Dr Taylor, I'm afraid of damaging my good knee if I go back to my regular physical activities or learning how to walk again, I might damage my good knee,' I say, despite all the positive affirmations of earlier on.

'But you can't live life afraid of damaging your knee all the time. If it breaks, we will fix it or better still, you can have a knee replacement. You cannot live your life trying to protect a good knee from breaking. It's better to live with a broken knee than to die with a good knee,' she says, and the penny dropped.

Oh my, gosh! Suddenly, the world has stopped spinning and I can hear the soundtrack to my own movie in the far distance. I need to live with a broken knee and not die with a good one. I am not God, and He has shown me that I am not Him and could never be. I am alive in this world with God as my protector, full of mercy and love, and He has given me the grace to live one day at a time according to His will. I am alive and it is time I start living. *Hooray! I can go ahead and break my good knee*, I think to myself with a broad smile.

I have spent so much time looking at what I have lost rather than looking at what I have gained. I lost a leg but I did not lose my life or myself. Why look at half-empty and half-full glasses when I can just look at the glass as it is and partake of whatever it contains? Why must I analyse and evaluate things constantly when I have so much? His grace is sufficient yet I chose to exist in insufficiency and in emotional and spiritual lack. Not any more, for I choose to live with a broken knee and not die with a good knee.

'Once upon a time, I dreamt I was a butterfly, fluttering hither and thither, to all intents and purposes a butterfly. I was conscious only of my happiness as a butterfly, unaware that I was myself. Soon I awaked, and there I was, veritably myself again. Now I do not know whether I was then a man dreaming I was a butterfly, or whether I am now a butterfly, dreaming I am a man.'

Zhuangzi[32]

CHAPTER TWENTY-THREE

A PIECE OF JEWELLERY

'Anything that's human is mentionable, and anything that is mentionable can be more manageable. When we can talk about our feelings, they become less overwhelming, less upsetting, and less scary. The people we trust with that important talk can help us know that we are not alone.'

Fred Rogers[33]

Another appointment to fit my prosthesis as the stump swelling continues to go down. Today, am getting a new socket so it's a long appointment.

'Good morning, Mrs Lethbridge,' says Catherine, my prosthetist, always smiling.

'Hello Catherine. How many times should I ask you to call me Mwangala? It's almost six months and we're stuck together for the rest of my life. Surely we're friends by now?' I ask her with a half-smile. 'Shall I wait in the ladies' waiting area?'

She nods in approval, still smiling. I've never caught her on a bad day, and I wheel myself to the ladies' area where it has the privacy I constantly seek. I am pleased the hospital has been considerate by providing such a facility.

It is there that I met Juliet, flipping through some outdated magazines, which she quickly discarded as I made myself as comfortable as I could. As we sat, Juliet kept babbling away and it soon became contagious and I caught her happy bug. I asked her how she managed to be so chirpy and positive in our seemingly dire dilemma. She let out a hearty laugh and said, 'Look at it like a piece of jewellery. It is just something you put on to look pretty, and you get on with your day. I just don't think about it.'

It was the best thing I had heard since my trauma, and then it slowly dawned on me that what I had or didn't have was not a loss after all. My prosthetic leg was an accessory which helped me navigate through the tunnel of my life in a much easier way. The physical pain that comes with wearing the prosthetic leg, especially when I was not yet used to it, was reminiscent of purchasing a shoe that I really liked in half a size too small. Squeezing my foot in hoping the leather would stretch. I may have looked good for the night but suffered for days afterwards. Oh, how blissful it could be if I could do that one more time.

My stump had to get used to the pressure of supporting my upper body, as I stood there like a stilt, all the while trying to make the prosthesis act like a foot. It required a conscious decision more than a reflexive action. These particular sessions were sometimes frustrating, especially since Catherine had to continue changing the sockets to get the right fit, as the stump continued to shrink in size. There was a time I had started to wonder whether there would ever be anything left by the time the shrinking was done. Therefore, I developed resentment towards 'no leg', but Catherine, forever optimistic with her beautiful smile, reassured me that all would be well.

The prosthesis, terribly similar to my 'Team Beach' long-lost oversized T-shirt, was comfortable but unfashionable. However, it has become a part of my dress code that I embrace and choose to wear. Unlike 'Team Beach', the prosthesis follows me to meetings and I must present myself accordingly in spite of everything else that is going on in my life.

It will become my accessory to life, just as I adorn myself with jewellery. I will get from point A to point B, with a determined swagger and the rest, as John would say, is simply a luxury.

'Un-winged and naked, sorrow surrenders its crown to a throne called grace.'

Aberjhani – The River of Winged Dreams[34]

CHAPTER TWENTY-FOUR

IT'S THERE IF YOU ASK

'In the depth of winter, I finally learned that within me there lay an invincible summer.'

Albert Camus[35]

'Mrs K?' I said, sobbing uncontrollably.

'Mokie, what's wrong? Why are you crying?' She can hear the despair in my voice.

'They had a class on the first floor, and there is no elevator. So, I did not attend the class. I failed to go to class,' I say to her in between sobs, dejected and helpless.

'Where are you?' she asked in clear panic.

'I'm at the corner of the road waiting for my Uber. I'm going back to the hotel,' I say.

The overwhelming fear and anxiety climb up my body and throat in an almost suffocating way. I lean over and bury my face into my lap, whilst I thank God that no one is around to see me weep.

'Mokie, go back there and ask, no, *tell* them you cannot use the stairs. Can't they see that you're in a wheelchair?' I can feel her agitation rising. Linda, my eldest sister, who has continued to assume a parental role that persistently casts me in the role of a child/ minor,[36] suddenly took over in her usual bossy manner. A personality trait I often resented, except for today.

'No, Mrs K, I'm scared.' Another thing I seem to have lost – my confidence. I am no longer as outspoken and strong-willed as I used to be.

'Mokie, if you do not go back right now, I'm calling the university, and I'm also calling the Disability Association because…' There's lots of shouting or I must have blacked her out because I can't register some of the things she's saying.

'… and I will also call…' She's still ranting and raving like wind across a field.

'Okay, please stop, I'm going back.'

I continue to plead with her in an attempt to calm her down. My tears are replaced by fear of my sister's wrath and the irreparable damage she might cause to new-found friendships by phoning the university. I am definitely more afraid of Linda than the lack of an elevator at the university block my lessons are in, so through a blur of motion and colour, I reluctantly wheel myself back towards the reception block and chastise myself for phoning her.

Arduously, I wheel myself back to the reception and, feeling rather foolish, I request the friendly lady at the desk for assistance to get to my class. One part of me is enraged, whilst the other wants to retreat to the confines of the hotel room, where I can cry myself to sleep, which was something I was better accustomed to. However, the other part of me doesn't want to explain myself to my elder sister if she asks how the issue was resolved. I know her, and like a dog with a bone, she will not let this go easily. Everything is surreal. After a few cowardly words, the receptionist suddenly realises the gravity of the school's oversight and profusely apologises and promises to rectify the anomaly. However, today's classes have already progressed and there is little that can be done. Oh, what relief I feel when I excuse myself and hurriedly propel myself towards the waiting Uber that will drive me back to the comfort of my hotel room.

It is a cold November morning and the Manchester city sky is grey and overcast. There is a slight drizzle and the wet autumn leaves that have fallen onto the sidewalk make it difficult to manoeuvre my wheelchair. So, I opt to use my prosthesis for the thirty-minute walk to the Business School building today. The biting wind whips around my face and I instinctively wrap my scarf tightly around my neck. Manchester, a vibrant, post-industrial gem at the heart of North West England, is a centre for culture and commerce and has the site of the world's oldest surviving passenger railway station. The city is immensely proud of its industrial past and of its influences on music and sport.[37] Still, here I am, wondering how and if the African in me will ever get used to the English cold.

That morning as I approach the Business School building, there is a notice on the door giving directions to the alternative rooms for the rest of our classes. They have been moved to a new building that has an elevator, and then I get a call from the Student Disability Office asking me to register with the association and I'm informed that they have arranged for me to have additional time to hand in my assignments, due to the side effects of my medication.

I felt a sudden flare of joy and could not contain my happiness. I broke into a broad smile at the thought of the extra time to hand in my assignments and felt like, finally, someone had thrown me a floatation ring, to spare me from my drowning. Mrs K was right: help is available when one asks for it. Oftentimes, I would shy away from asking people for small favours thinking that they were too busy to attend to my needs, or I would jump to the wrong conclusion that there were no facilities available for persons with disabilities in some establishments. *But of course, there were; this is the almighty University of Manchester and I am a student there*, I thought to myself, beaming with pride.

The reality is, when I ask for help, it is usually granted and given ungrudgingly. What may seem minute or irrelevant to an able-bodied person, could be something significant to a person with a disability, and this was the case for me. What were once mundane activities are now calculated movements, and in some cases things I can't do on my own. Therefore, there is nothing I receive without gratitude and I do not take for granted any kindness offered to me, for in my acceptance, I too have realised that I can exercise my independence.

Independence – my new-found word. With the passage of time, the word continues to morph into different things and different meanings. Is it just me that seeks the need for independence or are there other people battling with their own definition of the word and its meaning to their situation? I have stopped trying to figure it out because there is no generic answer that fits the different crosses we each have to bear. What I identified with as a person with a disability, is to be seen as I am and not as an object of misfortune. I am hopeful that the world will embrace me as I am and not as I was, for I have found that humanity's compassion has given me a 'glass half full' mentality.

The phantom pains remain steadfast in their path of disruption and do not follow my classroom timetable, especially since my pain relief medication insists on disrupting my concentration and reminding me that half empty is not full and not all the challenges I am facing are resolved. But that is simply called life.

'At any given moment you have the power to say: This is not how the story is going to end.'

Christine Mason Miller[38]

CHAPTER TWENTY-FIVE
PREGABALIN VS MBA

'Healing doesn't mean the damage never existed. It means the damage no longer controls our life.'

Akshay Dubey[39]

I am adjusting to a new country, a new environment, whose culture is a challenge I must deal with. The Master of Business Administration is a highly competitive degree. The curriculum is designed around ensuring that we gain a thorough understanding of value chain optimisation, as well as the ability to analyse situations and handle day-to-day problems.[40] It is demanding on most people but in my state, I find it to be double the challenge. On many occasions, due to the excessive workload, we have to work late into the night or sometimes way into the early hours of the morning, to be able to meet our presentation deadline the following day. The demand has taken a toll on me, and the need to take my medication at specific times means I have to manage my time well, as well as deal with the side effects.

The drowsiness weakens my focus, making me the weak link on a team that is full of talent. To make up for my apparent failure to effectively participate, I begin to work at awkward hours outside the team's scheduled time by ensuring that I cover the necessary topics and meet my targeted share of the workload throughout the night. Morning comes and upon taking my timed medication, I sit in class just to be counted as present because the side effects have kicked in. The lectures became background music that I have no control over, but I keep trying to understand the lyrics. The melody is pleasing and sounds more like the rustling of the yellowed leaves outside my window each morning.

Just as the Pregabalin wears off and the music stops, the professor's voice is becoming clear but the electric shock through my stump begins to rear its ugly head. It is time for more pain relief, which takes me back to the lulling music in the background that the professor was making earlier. It's now 7pm, the Pregabalin has worn off and my antenna stops picking up all the channels. Indeed, there is no rest for the wicked as the pain cycle makes its rounds.

I try my best to mask my discomfort because I want to integrate as much as I possibly can with my classmates. But being in a wheelchair one day and crutches on the next should have made me accept that there was no need for me try and act 'normal', for I was only disadvantaging myself in the process. These bizarre pain cycles cannot be hidden and the side effects of the medication cannot be ignored, however much I try to conceal them. I am using my need to integrate at my own peril, yet I could have easily asked for help.

I have now developed a routine of taking power naps to try and boost my energy levels, but the Pregabalin always seems to win. Fatigue has been building up, which has led me to being short-tempered and tearful. My room has become my refuge where I don't have to give a strong façade because anyone witnessing how I grab and squeeze my stump to ease the pain would think I'm acting like a crazy person. Especially since the pain doesn't select the most appropriate places to set off.

I am in the middle of a group session and my leg goes into spasms, and the electric shock reverberates from the phantom limb and sparks off at the tip of the stump. I scream internally, but my face is contorted from the excruciating pain as it shoots up into the remaining part of the leg. I look over to see if anyone has witnessed this and find Ben looking at me in concern. He pats my back as the lump in my throat begins to grow and I struggle to hold back their tears not knowing what to do.

'It's okay, Ben, I will be fine. Thank you,' I say in my most rehearsed, reassuring voice.

He tries hard to understand what is really going on but my expressions and tears are enough to tell what I am experiencing. The pain gradually eases as the pain relief takes effect.

Eventually, I have had to tell the university about what I am going through and am pleasantly surprised to find there are numerous support systems available to me. The university has a disability policy that allows me to take time off during sessions if and when the pain is unbearable enough to interrupt my class sessions. Additionally, my lecturers are informed of my limitations, which makes it easier for me to walk out mid-class sessions without appearing rude. Nevertheless, it now means my 'nine to five' has to change to 2am to 5am, necessitated by the heavy workload that comes with the MBA if I am to succeed.

Now it is all left to adapting to my situation and managing the side effects the best way I can. My reality and my desire are to complete the MBA by any means possible. If there was any other way of dealing with the side effects yet achieve my desired goal, I would have taken it, but there wasn't. I begin to question the reality I subjected myself to. Was all this really necessary? Did I really need this MBA? Why am I here freezing when I can be home watching *Greys Anatomy*[41] under my blankets? Whichever way, I cannot choose one over the other – Pregabalin or MBA? For today, the lack of sleep means I cannot decide. But it's 1-0 to Pregabalin.

'Courage doesn't always roar. Sometimes courage is the quiet voice at the end of the day saying, 'I will try again tomorrow.'

Mary Anne Radmacher[42]

CHAPTER TWENTY-SIX
NOT WELCOME HERE

'Welcome out of the cave, my friend, it's a bit colder out here, but the stars are just as beautiful.'

Plato[43]

There is an unwritten rule in most public spaces, boldly written in invisible ink, that states: 'Not Welcome Here'. There is no policy that dictates its presence, but there is no mistaking its existence. My first-hand experience of the 'Not Welcome Here' club was the misfortune of being turned away from a restaurant that my sister Lungowe had selected. Having Mwenda blood flowing through my veins, she knew that only food would convince me to leave the comfort of my veranda and subsequently, minimise the possibility of my falling into further despair.

'Hello uncles, *niza gena bwanji?*' I asked the gentleman we find at the entrance doors, enquiring how I would enter the restaurant seeing as there wasn't access for persons with disabilities.

The man takes a look at me, and then a quick glance at my wheelchair and calmly says, '*Ah ba antee, muyende chabe kwinangu,*' advising me to find another restaurant.

The covert policy excludes persons with disabilities not because they consciously discriminate against them, but there are striking similarities with the 'Right of Admission Reserved' policy except one is subject to interpretation and the other is based on qualification.

'Oh, okay uncles, thanks,' and I urge my sister to push me back to the car, but she wouldn't have it.

Once upon a time, I was the outspoken advocate of injustice and prejudice, yet in this instance, I felt helpless as I watched my sister take on the fight on my behalf with the 'uncles'. Her frantic shouts were attracting attention and I didn't want to be the centre of attention. I asked her to let it be and just leave because all the ranting and justifications were making me tired. With my confidence eroded already, it left me feeling only one kind of way – wanting to go home to the safety of my veranda. I couldn't help my sister fight that particular battle as I was still fighting one huge elephant in my room called acceptance. How could I advocate for the persons with disabilities when I was still struggling to admit to myself, let alone say it out loud, that I was a part of the marginalised group? I had to reserve my energy to fight another day.

I spent the remainder of my days on my veranda asking *Ba* Diana, my carer, for bottomless tea while watching the birds destroy my palms.

I felt lost because the place I called home and had dreamed about with all the wonderful memories I cherished suddenly alienated me, and I found myself yearning for the country I had reluctantly adopted. I was saddened that I felt out of place in my own country, but I had to accept and find peace with it, regardless of what was presented to me.

While I feel the welfare of persons with disabilities is a national obligation, it is evident and quite clear that care and compassion is a voluntary and individual attribute rather than a compulsory subject. What is said in the policy documents is significantly at odds with the 'Not Welcome Here' silent policy. Personally, I yearn for systems to be put in place that can help me get back to as 'normal' a life as I practicably can, and which would allow me to participate as fully as I possibly can in my society without feeling as though I have a problem, or worse still, that I am the problem.

Being home after wanting so badly to return to the place where I'd had my last happy memory, only to find the first restaurant I went to applying the 'Not Welcome Here' silent policy, was a rude and unpleasant shock. It was a clear indication that the restaurant did not have any provision for persons with disabilities in their establishment, and I was certain it was common practice in many more such establishments.

I am still not certain if the silent coding was the worst thing ever as, with time, as I began to venture beyond the comfort of my veranda, I began to encounter different types of responses people had towards my predicament.

I once went to one of the many shopping malls in Lusaka and asked the car park attendant to remove the plastic cone that blocked the disabled parking slot. He peered inside my car and said in fragmented Nyanja, '*Nanga imwe muli na disabled?*' checking whether I *had* a disability. I came out of the car and felt his stare on my back as I deliberately gave my worst ever walk whilst holding onto my sticks in an exaggerated 'I am about to die' kind of way and left him standing there silently. When I got back and found him standing by my car, I was upset that he had the audacity to 'look after' my car, especially after being so rude, but instead, he fell to his knees cried out loudly,

'*Amayi ni khululukileni. Amayi sinenzo'ziba. Amayi mweo mulungu!*' he pleaded, beseeching God's mercy.

Whilst on his knees he almost held me by my legs, but thankfully chose to tug at my *chitenge* traditional wrap. He put his hands together as if in prayer and continued to plead with me in the local dialect, '*Njeleleniko, Lesa akankanda efyo namichita!*' fearing God's wrath on his soul.

I wondered what people must imagine disability was and whether they only had to see it to believe it. I recalled all the signage in the UK that read: 'Remember, not all disabilities are visible', and was upset that, in Zambia, the guard had to put his head into my car to confirm my state, which he still couldn't establish with my traditional wrapper on. My walking aids became my much-needed evidence.

'Not Welcome Here' is a catastrophe which needs to be addressed and laid to bare, otherwise persons with disabilities will constantly be the marginalised sector of society with no recourse except to keep their chins up and take the blows with no defence. Policies are in abundance, but if there is no sound implementation, they are not worth the paper they are written on. Society needs to understand that most people with disabilities do not appreciate the political correctness that surrounds the various limitations we have towards numerous activities, for not only do I think it's silly and impersonal, but there is a definite need for society to be more empathetic towards us. *Not Welcome Here* should read as *All are Welcome Here*.

'Part of the problem with the word "disabilities" is that it immediately suggests an inability to see or hear or walk or do other things that many of us take for granted. But what of people who can't feel? Or talk about their feelings? Or manage their feelings in constructive ways? What of people who aren't able to form close and strong relationships? And people who cannot find fulfilment in their lives, or those who have lost hope, who live in disappointment and bitterness and find in life no joy, no love? These, it seems to me, are the real disabilities.'[44]

Fred Rogers

CHAPTER TWENTY-SEVEN

GETTING BETTER

'You've made a new friend. You say you're going in the backyard soon. You're getting better, kiddo.'
'Please don't say that.'
'Why not? Why shouldn't we celebrate it?'
'Because it's just too much, okay? It's not that big a deal.'
'It's big enough,' she said. 'Who knows, in a few years you could be ready to face the world again.'
'Trust me,' he said. 'It's not a switch I can turn on and off, Grandma.'[45]

John Corey Whaley – Highly Illogical Behaviour[46]

The process of getting better is not just a moment or an event or a decision you make once and hope that it is final. Getting better is never-ending motion. It is walking, it is effort, it is a conscious state of activities that can sometimes be painful, and usually, not comfortable. It is personal endurance and prayer for change and acceptance, especially after hard negotiations with both man and God. The energy that remains, if any, is now channelled towards the desire to get better physically, mentally, and spiritually.

I recall the loss of my first political campaign as a member of parliament as being bittersweet. I lost partly because I sat there passively thinking that my decision to stand was a win in itself. I had made the decision to stand against a strong incumbent and then forgot that I needed to walk as well as surround myself with campaign team members who held my vision for the constituency. I thought standing alone was sufficient. Needless to say, it was not.

There were many lessons I learnt through that election experience, and going through my healing process now feels akin to the feeling I had during that loss, looking ahead to how I will reposition myself in the political arena in future: two battle fronts with similar rules of engagement to achieve intended goals. I lost one battle the first time, but I intend to win the other. I need to get better and win this battle whatever it takes.

So, mantras like '*Walk with me if you must, pass me even, and I will not complain. In fact, I will be in awe of you. But please, do not ask me to stop and wait for you for I will keep walking, with or without you*' by my close friend Dr Usha, which were shoved down my throat as dessert, after our lunches comprising solely of Indian starters, became a greater part of my life – adapting such principles and, unfortunately or fortunately, the words came to mean exactly that to me in a literal sense.

I needed to keep walking, and I will have to keep walking because no one will wait for me. This is my moment of reflection and suddenly it all makes sense to me. In getting better, I need to look at the primary object that will walk the walk – me.

I am now standing, but the shake in my shoulder will not go away even when I try to stand still. The doctors told me earlier that the broken right femur needs movement to encourage calcification, the process in which calcium builds up in the body tissue causing it to harden. My 'remodelled' left knee needs me to use common sense in how I exert pressure onto it, so as not to injure it further. It now feels as though the doctors are playing a secret game of 'how will she create that movement?' Nonetheless, there was something genuinely nice, in an indulgent kind of way, about letting other people handle things for you, but the time to get back into my old life work schedule finally arrived. Butterflies fill my stomach, but what better way is there than to jump into the deep end and take a long drive to Solwezi from Lusaka with my boys. The trip to Solwezi to inspect one of the construction sites is an opportunity to bond with my boys. Nina, on the other hand, has chosen to travel to Hong Kong to do Hong Kong stuff with her former school mate who lives there and who has kindly invited Nina to spend part of the summer holiday with her family.

We reach the end of the road and check into one of the hotels. Despite it being one of the top hotels in the area, there is no room for the disabled, which surprises me somewhat, but they are very apologetic and offer to bring me a makeshift shower stool I can use. We settle for two ordinary rooms with ordinary shower facilities as none of the rooms have bathtubs (phew!) or showers with fixed shower stools. They bring me a plastic garden chair to sit on while I shower. Well, the heaviness of my weight spreads the fragile chair legs into four different directions like a compass trying to show me which way is north. The slippery floor only makes the poor thing groan even more under my weight when it can't find a ledge to hook its spindly legs onto.

After carefully balancing myself against the shower partitions to support my frame, I realise the only way to avoid slipping and ending up in a rural clinic with a burst knee would be to sit myself onto the shower floor on all the towels I could find. Finally seated, I force myself to cry, but not a single tear comes my way. The truth is, although I feel drained and humiliated, this is the most ridiculous position I've found myself in and I collapse into laughter.

I certainly cannot cry about everything I encounter along life's path; challenges are my status quo. Whatever happens, I simply need to get on with it, adapt, find my own rhythm, and dance (or sit) to the sound of my continuously playing mental music. Zambia doesn't seem to have fully integrated the needs of persons with disabilities in general, based on my experiences. The public transport system and the social amenities are primary on the list of unequal access to gain entry. This leaves persons with disabilities like me having to adapt to the challenges we face which, in retrospect, applies to everyone.

'Mwangala, stop standing there with a wobble and shake; it is time to walk!' I chide myself.

'You gain strength, courage and confidence by every experience in which you really stop to look fear in the face. You are able to say to yourself, "I have lived through this horror. I can take the next thing that comes along." You must do the thing you think you cannot do.'

Eleanor Roosevelt[47]

CHAPTER TWENTY-EIGHT

AUTHENTIC

'Give yourself permission to let it hurt but also allow yourself the permission to let it heal.'

Nikki Rowe[48]

I have done countless hours of yoga and meditation, and numerous hours of introspection in the dark of the early morning as half the world sleeps on, asking myself and the universe the same question: how can I be authentic, or rather, how can I be present in a situation when there is a permanent sadness in my soul? People go through difficult situations like we all do, but for some, more challenging than others, which requires them to make hard decisions to even walk away from their loved ones and disappear to find their authentic selves. They put on hard faces that betray their families largely for their own survival to avoid being swallowed by someone's deep dark hole. That sense of permanent sadness is like a whirlpool that sucks everything in its vicinity. It is vicious and intense; it seeks solitude.

In his book *Leadership BS: Fixing Workplaces and Careers One Truth at a Time*, Jeffrey Pfeffer's[49] description of the loss of his friend's daughter captures the very essence of what I am feeling and have been feeling. He says: 'The experience of losing a daughter is part of my soul, a sadness I will never get over…' Trying to get on with my studies in business school, flashing the toothy smile at work, dealing with clients I consider difficult, and then handling the different emotional states of my family at home as an authentic mother and wife for the people who matter the most in my life, are all shifting emotions I have perfected to suit particular situations. In many instances, I feel like a fraudster for being able to have the capacity to fake various emotions. Of all the people I have to deal with, my children and my husband need me the most, and yet I find myself faking my smile to them the most.

As per usual, I am in my room crying when my door bursts open and it is AJ, again, and I raise my voice at him. He has caught me unawares and I try to compose myself to hide from him the emotional breakdown I am going through. It feels like a different kind of emotional surge that has swept over me. I quickly chase him out of my room reprimanding him at the same time. It isn't really about the not knocking that bothers me but the sense of 'nakedness' he has found me in. I am vulnerable and didn't have the chance to 'put on my mask' before he entered. I don't want him to be a witness to my anguish; after all, he is only a child. He retreats, which gives me a few seconds to 'put on my face'.

'Knock, knock!', he shouts in an exaggerated manner behind the closed door. It is rather comical the way he does it because he is demonstrating what he has been instructed to do.

'Who is it?' I say calmly, as though I don't know who it is.

'It's AJ,' he shouts.

'Come in,' I shout even louder to give him the impression I am glad to let him in.

'Mom, could I please buy some V-bucks?' he asks as he runs in excited with the warm welcome. Instead, I lecture him on the need to save all we can and not spend money online unwisely. He listens to me intently though I am unsure he wants to hear this lecture right now. Despite everything, I say I will oblige him just this once, and as soon as he leaves the room, I lock the door behind him, take off 'my face', and weep.

It is a continuation of part one of the tears, but it is also that I don't even know what V-bucks are! I was admonishing my son lovingly over the infamous V-bucks that I don't even know, but it seemed like something I needed to say to him then, and I am back to questioning myself all over again, questioning my authenticity. It is a roller coaster of emotions I cannot contain. Much as I'm desperate to jump off this ferris wheel, I become more curious to understand what V-bucks are and, wiping away the remainder of my tears, I ask Siri to help me out.

There is no right answer to my self-posed questions, but all I know is that, over time, I have perfected the art of 'putting on my face' to suit the situation. It has become my coping mechanism, and one I need not understand – no one should. What matters to me most is that with each 'face' there is some part that is authentic. 'Putting on the face' means survival and a way of dealing with every circumstance that requires my compassion, intellect and dedication.

In my struggle to provide a sense of normalcy and the stability my kids need in their life, I must wear the 'strong' mom face they are familiar with. I make every effort I can to prevent them from reliving the ordeal of the looped clip of my brokenness. I need them to see me triumph over my challenges, and I can't subject them to the slow turning wheels of nature, at least for the time being.

I find it comforting though when I simply switch off my internal conflict in order to survive a present situation, and then later, in the privacy of my own space, I am myself again and this is where I am truly authentic. There is only one person for whom I cannot put on the face – my husband. He sees me as I am. Nothing seems to faze him or suggest he sees me differently other than the weight I see on his shoulders. Perhaps it is from him being English or maybe it is just his personality that makes him see things differently from most, I don't know. He would find me crying and softly say, 'Oh babe,' as he squeezed me gently, rocking me from side to side in silence. A few moments later, he'd say, 'Why don't I go and make us a cup of tea?', more as statement than a question. The door closes gently behind him and I hear him shout: 'Boys, two minutes, we're going to the park.' It's his way of letting me be authentic in private with no one around to look at me.

Hours later, hugging my pillow, there sits on the nightstand my cold cup of tea.

'Authenticity is not the search for uniqueness. An oak tree does not try to become an oak tree. A cactus does not try to become a cactus. All living things simply reach for nourishment – they reach for sun, reach for water, reach their roots deeper into the ground. By being open to receiving what they need, they become unique effortlessly. So, let yourself fall open. Forget about crafting yourself a unique personality. Just allow. Allow in love. Allow pain. Allow desire. Allow learning. Allow healing. Allow frustration. Allow uncertainty. Allow yourself to experience what you must experience and learn what you need to learn, so that your uniqueness can emerge organically.'

Vironika Tugaleva

CHAPTER TWENTY-NINE

NUMBERS

'History, despite its wrenching pain, cannot be unlived, but if faced with courage, need not be lived again.'

Maya Angelou[50]

The number one will always be the number one, in any language, whether or not it is created by an individual or gathered by a qualitative study. What changes is the interpretation of what the number one means to everyone. I often wonder what the story is behind the number one, and what narrative the interpreter would have to change the narrative.

I have one leg, I lost one leg. In whichever instance, both statements are true. So, which story am I going to tell the world, and more importantly, what do I believe to be true? Do I have one leg or have I lost one leg? I don't know; I'm still trying to figure it all out. Some days, I wake up without one leg and I listen to Kiana Lede's 'One of Those Days'[51] and I'm the only person supplying the drinks to my pity-party, then the next day, I wake up with one leg and I listen to CeCe Winans' 'Mercy Said No'[52] and I am cognisant of God's grace over my life. The commonality in both days is that they're tear-filled and emotive where I exist in parallel realities.

'Lord, when will it stop being one of those days?' For me, the narrative is undefined because there is a thin line between joy and sadness – just this grey area of existence that doesn't want to subsect with the other. I look at my prosthetic leg and the grey tights I'm wearing, which seem to fit the narrative of the grey part of my existence, and today's song on the playlist is Katelyn Tarver's 'You Don't Know'.[53] I have to accept this to be my new reality, but I don't embrace it, however much I try. Instead, I have learned to live with it because, whichever way, one is one in any language, and it has immediate relevance to my current situation.

'I'm lying, yes, but why do you force me to give a linear explanation; linear explanations are almost always lies.'

Elena Ferrante[54]

CHAPTER THIRTY

THE SMALL PRINT

'You may have to fight a battle more than once to win it'.

Margaret Thatcher[55]

Commode, wheelchair, banana board, hand support, amputee socks, two-centimetre heel, three-centimetre heel – any centimetre heel, Tramadol, oral morphine, Senna, Gabapentin, Pregabalin, hypovolemic shock, below knee, above knee, double amputee, bacteria, bed rest, bed rest, and even more wretched bed rest. Terms and conditions suddenly have a whole new meaning to me; terminology of equipment I have come to understand and learn of as well as familiar terms of the condition of my body. These are now my new terms and conditions, but what is the small print here? What does it actually say? This is what catches my attention when I least expect it, and often never in my favour. The small print says: 'Once you have lost a limb, it is not replaceable and it is non-refundable – it is gone.'

The rehabilitation sessions have continued almost relentlessly, and I have been taught by my physiotherapist how to sit on the floor from the bed despite having learnt how to do it accidentally with the green creature the first time. I sit on the edge of the bed then gently drop onto a step, and then drop on to the floor. I have been left alone momentarily for the physiotherapist to attend to the other patients in the class. I am weakened by the fast during Lent. I am reminded of Welu's words when he said to me many Lenten periods ago that, when I am hungry and weak, I should pray. I try to pray, but each time I am reminded that I cannot kneel. So, I lie on my blue mat surrounded by my fellow amputees, and I begin to silently groan. It is an indistinct guttural noise that I hope my God will understand because I can't verbalise the words I want to say. 'Somebody, anybody, can you hear me? Please lay me at His feet.' I am here mourning the loss of my leg. I want my leg back; I want my old life back: 'Why me, Lord, why me?' I moan silently, hoping that no one will witness the pain and anguish of my Lamentation.

I lay there and rolled myself onto my side, and quietly buried my face in the floor mat and wept. I cried for everything. I cried for my mother, I cried for my children, I cried for my husband, I cried for my old life, and then I wept for the loss of my leg. There was no other way I could do it other than how I knew best. Now I am weeping for all that and more. How can I not be allowed to scream and mourn for my loss? I have not been given a chance to mourn my 'death' – my loss. Why am I expected to act strong and appear everywhere with a brave face and calm disposition as though it is my second nature? When in fact, when home alone in the dead of night and everyone is asleep, I cry. I am alone and there is no one crying on the floor with me – just lots of prayers, lots of 'you're lucky to be alive', and lots of statements that begin with 'at least…' Who said I feel lucky to be alive? Who said I want to be prayed for in order for me to find peace and healing in those dark moments when I need to mourn? 'At least' what? Please tell me, 'at least' what? My pain is palpable, and I feel the loss I have suffered. The statements and words of encouragement are all said with good intentions except the best support I need in these moments of meltdown is the gift of silence.

I wait each day for someone to come through my bedroom door and shout, 'Taa-daaa, here is your leg – I was just joking,' but with each passing day, it slowly dawns on me that the joke really is on me. No one is going to bring back my leg. I prayed and prayed, and everyone around me prayed even harder. I asked God to take the burden away from me even as I quoted scripture after scripture of healing, thinking that if my sins were too grave for a miracle, then surely someone among the people that were praying for me would be one soul worthy of His ear. He did reassure Abraham that He would save Gomorrah if there were one person who was righteous. So why not me? These are the modern days and people seem to have greater faith now than they did then. There ought to have been one soul whose prayer should have been heard, but I realise God doesn't operate that way. I needed to read even the fine print in scripture, but I could not find the terms of reference, and as far as I was concerned, God had turned His back on me.

'My Lord and my God, why have you forsaken me?' had a whole new meaning for me when I felt abandoned and alone. I pushed myself to praise His name even when the fight seemed lost and hope was waning. I sought encouragement from everything godly I could think of, and tried to find peace in my situation, but there I was hurting senselessly when praise eventually seemed far from my lips. Big mistake! What I didn't realise was that I was trying to lean on the understanding and wisdom of man, yet only God can give absolute peace in any situation. Every inspired word I read was only motivational without addressing the root cause of my discouragement and despair. In my state, I may have been angry with God and ultimately undermined His sovereignty as I lost my focus on His grace and mercy. Yet, it was in my feeling of abandonment that I found His abundance.

But right now, I need to weep, and I do it the only way I know how. I weep as we do in Zambia when we mourn for the loss of our loved ones and cast away all our creature comforts by sitting on the floor and cover our heads with a *duku* and wrap *chitenge* cloth around our waists. I find that by expressing ourselves in this way, sitting on the floor in cleared house spaces during funerals while the men sit outside in the cold around a fire, we find healing of sorts. We could all choose to just turn up for the burial if we liked, but we don't. Instead, we sit on the floor and weep for all that's lost, in the same way that I now weep for what I have lost.

Pain and loss have a strange way of forming concepts and ideas that influence the mind. I actualised what I presumed to be true about what God really thought of me and I thought that He found a way of punishing me. Yet, He was there with me through all my tribulation and never judged me based on my thoughts. My perception was not God's, and neither were the motivational and encouraging messages I was reading and receiving. God had a plan for me that I may not have acknowledged then because my mind was focused on my pain, but He was there with me and He waited. Now I look back and realise I did feel His presence, but it was not how I wanted Him to present Himself to me. I had my own expectations because I wanted Him to intervene in my life the way I wanted Him to. Oh, how man minimises God!

Just as we weep for the souls of our lost loved ones, we also cry out to God and ask Him to give us back our child, give someone back her husband, our friend, our parents, our anyone that we hold near and dear – just give them all back, but, after a few days, we bury our loss and leave the grave, and then try to pick up the pieces. What I have come to realise now is that we never really get over our losses. We merely learn to live with them because we can never stop mourning the loss of a loved one, just as I will never stop mourning the loss of my leg. I never had the chance to bury my loss. I woke up and it was gone. So, I lie here on this blue mat surrounded by strangers and murmur the lyrics of Tameela Manns' 'Take Me to The King'.[56]

'Truth is I'm tired, options are few. I'm trying to pray, but where are you?
... Take me to the king. I don't have much to bring. My heart's torn to pieces. It's my offering...
No tears to cry, even if I tried.
But still, my soul refuses to die'.

I want to scream out as hard and as loudly as I possibly can for the world to see and hear that I am in mourning, and I am hurting, and I crave God's presence so that He can finally hear my cry. I want the world to acknowledge what and how I feel, but I also know there are so many people who are lucky to be alive – and so am I. A lot of people don't make it; they breathe their last breath, yet I lived to take one more having been brought back from the edge. I stop and ponder on the thought that maybe I, too, should have died. I carry some form of guilt for being alive. I have lost my friends in motorbike accidents, friends that used to be our support riders to Siavonga. They died in similar crashes that saw me come out of alive. So, how can I cry when there are people in worse-off situations than mine? But who weighs the gravity of being allowed to express grief? What is the scale I should use so that I can stop acting strong, and really just sit on the floor and cry out to God and declare that I just want my old life back?

The floor has given me the much-needed opportunity I have sought to express my loss. Gradually, peace comes over me and I welcome the mental exhaustion that has inadvertently sent me to sleep. A gentle touch on my shoulder rouses me from my slumber.

'Mwangala, your transport is here, are you ready to go home?' my physiotherapist says to me.

I nod my head and smile. I have made it – one day at a time. I have lived through it and I am alive. I will live to fight another day, but for now, let me just live.

'If you don't know my pain, then you will never understand my praise.'

Juanita Bynum[57]

CHAPTER THIRTY-ONE

SADNESS

The nutritionist said I should eat root vegetables.
Said if I could get down thirteen turnips a day
I would be grounded, rooted.
Said my head would not keep flying away
to where the darkness lives.

The psychic told me my heart carries too much weight.
Said for twenty dollars she'd tell me what to do.
I handed her the twenty. She said, 'Stop worrying, darling.
You will find a good man soon.'

The first psychotherapist told me to spend
three hours each day sitting in a dark closet
with my eyes closed and ears plugged.
I tried it once but couldn't stop thinking
about how gay it was to be sitting in the closet.

The yogi told me to stretch everything but the truth.
Said to focus on the out breath; said everyone finds happiness
when they care more about what they give
than what they get.

The pharmacist said, 'Lexapro, Lamictal, Lithium, Xanax.'

The doctor said an anti-psychotic might help me
forget what the trauma said.

The trauma said, 'Don't write these poems.
Nobody wants to hear you cry
about the grief inside your bones.'

But my bones said, 'Tyler Clementi jumped
from the George Washington Bridge
into the Hudson River convinced
he was entirely alone.'

My bones said, 'Write the poems.'

Andrea Gibson, 'The Madness Vase'[58]

Today is my sisters Notulu's (Noti's) birthday, and as a birthday gift to her, I have decided to dedicate today's session of 'all day in bed' especially to her. I can't move however much I try; I am paralysed by something that has weakened me, which I can't put my finger on. I must simply be tired I suppose, with everything that's going around and within me. My cousin Nomai, who lives in the picturesque town of Canterbury, had phoned earlier to ask me to confirm if it was indeed Noti's birthday. She hears the sadness in my voice and quickly realises this one-sided conversation needs a polite way to end. She gives me one last piece of advice in the hope that my spirit is lifted.

'You know, Mwangala, you need to remember that what you are going through is simply in the meantime,' she says in a calm, calculated way, knowing there is no easy way of dealing with my turmoil.

There are people everywhere fighting their own private battles, while trying to make sense of what is going on around them, in the 'in the meantime' phase of their lives. Most people probably have burdens of sorts that they carry. Perhaps, the difference lies in how we carry them single-handedly as individuals or collectively as a family. So sad that I am not alone in my 'in the meantime' struggle – neither do I find comfort in the realisation that I am not weak, unusual or insane.

My burdens overpower me today and have left me sprawled across my bed like a donkey that has collapsed under its heavy load, lying helpless, stretched out and unable to move. But I need to get up and change my story so that I too can be that person that got up and walked. I have become accustomed to the silent treatment that my God has been giving me. However, today is different as He has surprised me with a response. I hear Him as clearly as I see the blue Lusaka sky my heart yearns for. I cannot doubt the clarity of His response.

'Lord, when will I stop writing about all this sadness?' I ask.

'When you stop being sad,' He declares.

'Come to me, all who labour and are heavy laden, and I will give you rest. Take my yoke upon you, and learn from me, for I am gentle and lowly in heart, and you will find rest for your souls. For my yoke is easy, and my burden is light.'

Matthew 11:25-30[59]

CHAPTER THIRTY-TWO
TEN SECONDS

'The function of prayer is not to influence God, but rather to change the nature of the one who prays.'

Soren Kierkegaard

'Lent is a special time of prayer, penance, sacrifice and good works in preparation of the celebration of Easter.'[60] It is a time for penance and, as a Catholic having observed this time over the years, this year seems more important to me because it is a time for me to hear God's word. I need to hear Him because I have not heard him for the last few months. So perhaps there has been too much noise. So, this Lenten time of silence and devotion to prayer may provide me the opportunity I seem to have missed to hear Him.

It is day sixteen of fasting during Lent and I am left wondering how Jesus managed to fast for forty days. Yes, granted He *is* Jesus, but surely, if others can make it then there is no excuse for any God-fearing faithful person to do the same. I am God-fearing, that I am certain of, but is my lack of faith causing me to get cross-eyed? The white lilies on the sill of my window are beginning to look a lot more like ice cream. The stack of books meant to occupy my recovery time has a semblance of a freshly baked loaf; as the aroma fills my nostrils my mouth begins to water and I am immediately transported back in time to a simpler life. I remember watching my father baking bread with my siblings. We sat there on the floor of the kitchen peering through the glass panel of the stove, watching the dough rise as it slowly turned brown. The aroma seeps through the oven door, filling the house and I can already taste the flavour of the melted butter on the hot thick slices we all got. We hear the pulsating sound of my father's footsteps and we quickly scamper away to find hiding places.

'Go away, I got to the curtain first,' and an elbow shoves me out of the drapes as I instantly fall to the ground. There is no time to cry, I must find a hiding place before Dad finds me, otherwise I will surely not get my share. I scramble away and hide my head under the coffee table and cover my face with my hands; the rest of body sticking out like a sore thumb does not worry me, for my childlike mind believes that if I cannot see him then he must not be able to see me either. The memory makes me smile because Dad would indeed pretend not to see me. I call out to the universe silently, 'Somebody please tell me that hallucinations are part of fasting,' then slowly reach out for Dr Myles Monroe's book

Fasting 101 – How to Fast Efficiently, looking for a part on hallucinations during fasting, if that chapter exists. Instead, I find where he wrote that: 'Fasting does not move God. We fast to give us capacity to allow God to move us.'[61] So, I whisper a prayer, 'Lord, I choose to wait upon you, for strength to last the duration of Lent and the strength to survive this trying time of my life.'

It is often said that it is only when you lose something that you realise its importance. One leg gone and there goes my ability to walk and stopping myself from rolling over in the bathtub – a simple pleasure I took for granted. I have to go through more physiotherapy sessions, and this time, it is to train my right arm to move. Slowly, I try to touch my chin, and I hear, 'No, Mwangala, do not bring your chin down to your hand.' *Oh dear, she saw me*, is my immediate thought as I supress a smile. After all, I'm so accustomed to being miserable that smiling feels like a guilty pleasure, but it is a welcome emotion that I have missed.

Then weeks later, it is bringing the hand toward my nose and then to my forehead. They tell me the day I touch my forehead is the day I get discharged from the rehabilitation ward. Really – touch my forehead! How could such a simple task become a determinant of whether I stay in the rehab clinic or not? How could something so mundane become a major factor in my healing process? Yet every part of my body hurts doing that, and for the first time since the crash, I curse the unknown driver that did this to me. I have never wanted to know his identity. Unknown to my family and friends, it has caused me to wonder each time I am in Zambia when I see a man – any man – and I ask myself silently, 'Is it you?' What torment, and still, I refuse to know who he is.

The physio team is relentless in my rehabilitation process, and the amputee clinic is teaching me how to strengthen my glutes in readiness for the prosthetic leg. I religiously attend the amputee weekly clinics, and I sit quietly observing how others cope with their circumstances. It is a moment of awe and wonder imagining what they could have gone through to get them here, and whether their situations were better or worse than mine. I can't help but marvel at their tenacity and their will to overcome their challenges.

Tea break offers me an opportunity to investigate further. I ask the 'guys' what their stories are, and each has his own to tell, but they all have one thing in common; they do not mind their prosthetic legs because 'It's awesome,' says one, and 'It has high-performance chips,' says another. 'But why not have a leg that looks real with all the new technology,' I ask? Their responses are varied and none gives me the solace I seek. I just want to get my life back and wear a prosthetic that doesn't transform.

Whilst in rehab, I realise that there are no black amputees except me. Am I the only black girl living in the UK that has lost her leg? The sessions which are meant to be helpful leave me more confused and questioning. I suddenly feel lost. Forget about being the only girl; I am the only black amputee in the clinic while I am here, but I suppose I should be relieved as this is not really the place where I ought to seek familiarity for the sake of comfort. I am also the only person who wants a normal-looking prosthesis that looks as much as possible like my other leg. I am not interested in performance. All I need is function, and since I obviously cannot have my old leg back, I want the new one to trick my mind into believing it is back.

Several hospital trips and lots of pain relief later, my stump finally heals enough to put my thigh into some moonwalker suit which they pump with air to give me support. My thoughts immediately take me to a petrol station, but Gail's question whether the pressure is enough brings me back to reality. She pulls me up and places my elbows on the arm rest at chest level and I stand for ten seconds. Ten full seconds, and just as gently as she pulled me up, Gail supports me to sit on the edge of the bed.

When you lose a part of you, the smallest and most unassuming bits of action open the floodgates of tears. No, I am not hormonal; it is sadness filled with exhilarating joy. Finally, the wretched light at the end of the infamous tunnel that everyone talks about shimmers through my tears, and there it is – the possibility of being able to walk again. I have stood for ten full seconds!

'Being in a hurry. Getting to the next thing without fully entering the thing in front of me. I cannot think of a single advantage I've ever gained from being in a hurry. But a thousand broken and missed things, tens of thousands, lie in the wake of all the rushing... Through all that haste I thought I was making up time. It turns out I was throwing it away.'

**Ann Voskamp – One Thousand Gifts:
A Dare to Live Fully Right Where You Are**[62]

CHAPTER THIRTY-THREE

PHYSIO, PHYSIO, AND SO MUCH MORE PHYSIO

'Stop the pity party! Your sorrow is full and complete when you go through unfortunate circumstances and decide to mourn for life as a result of the unexpected.'

Israelmore Ayivor[63]

It's the same drive, along the same route, at a constant 30mph and I'm securely wrapped at the back of the hospital transport in my wheelchair. It's a routine I have become accustomed to undertaking three times a week. There is an aria playing in the background and my thoughts go to whether or not it is possible to have a physiotherapy overdose. All these sessions I have been having don't seem to have relieved the tiredness and anger I feel. It appears no one is listening to me. It is physio, then the wheelchair, then more physio, and then asking for another cup of tea. I get angry from my inability to control my life and care for myself and my family. The frustration, irritation and anger I feel in most cases unfortunately ends up affecting the people I love the most – my family. I can't stop feeling all these negative emotions and all this turmoil within me, but I know I need to snap out of it very soon before I totally hurt the very same family I begged God to let me live for. Maybe what is need is a psychiatrist and not physio. My thoughts are suddenly interrupted by the driver's voice.

'What happened?' Steve asks me when he comes to pick me up for my umpteenth physio session. He turns the volume down as I proceed to narrate the pity-party story. If he can ask the question, it means I have the right to tell it the way I deem fit, especially to a willing audience.

'I guess this is my life now. I simply have to accept it,' I say somewhat indifferently when I do not elicit the empathy I seek from him. *Why isn't he joining me in my pity-party?* I question myself.

I have grown comfortable with people telling me how sorry they are, and how I should hold my head up because I am a strong woman. I am tired though of putting on different faces to suit different circumstances and people. I can't voice out all the things I feel, but telling someone any version of what I feel could relieve the tension I bottle up, which could create some room to fill with pleasant thoughts, but his response startles me as he's having none of the drinks I am serving at my pity party.

'You don't live with it; it lives with you,' he says with a grin on his face. This is unexpected and it doesn't fit into my defined narrative.

Steve was diagnosed with multiple sclerosis (MS), a disease in which the immune system attacks the protective covering of nerves, potentially disabling the brain and the central nervous system in the spine. He explains how MS has lived with him for twenty odd years. I'm thinking he must have made an error in his explanation and doesn't really mean the MS I think I know, but he says it again: 'I don't have MS. MS merely lives with me.'

He chats on happily as though he's talking about a rudimentary tooth extraction, and I can see he is serious. I am dumbfounded though a little disappointed upon realising he is not going to buy the drinks to the pity-party, and he is dealing with an irreversible medical condition. He's speaking with such energy that I am left with only one thing to do – turn off the music and thank him.

The *enemy* has tried to isolate me from my loved ones, and I have reached near breaking point. I fell into a depressed state of mind, refusing to speak to anyone and pushing them away and, in most cases, seeking quietness and solitude. Yet, here is Steve who should have happily jumped into my song and dance and yet chose not to. Instead, he drives me home with such zest for life that I look down at the prosthesis on my lap, then slowly close my eyes and whisper to it: 'I do not live with my leg; my leg lives with me.'

I have learnt a great lesson, that being disabled does not make me less of a person, and I am not in the outer court as I had imagined. I am still in the inner court, wonderfully and fearfully made by God my creator, who has shown me His mercy. I was whole yet I chose to live such an unfulfilled life. I had His grace and mercy fully bestowed upon me, yet I chose to live at half-mast. The question remains, what did I seek before the ordeal? There is no single answer that would adequately provide closure to the endless 'what if' scenarios that went through my mind as we all choose different paths in life to make the most of the 'what if' outcome of the opportunities life provides us.

Admittedly, I have learnt to push through the pain and appreciate each emotion that stirs within me. I have learnt to live with a spirit of gratitude and not despair, seeing that I did not die but lived. I have accepted myself as I am, and have discovered parts of myself that I never embraced before. I want to learn how to be brave despite the turmoil that is going on within me, which I cannot explain to most, but enough such that I tell myself I am not done yet. There is more I can still achieve if only I can face another day. My bravery is not for other people to see and to applaud my strength and courage, but it's rather for myself to be able to move beyond the pain of the trauma and see what God has in store for me.

I look back and understand that my plans are not God's plans. When I think I have it all figured out, sometimes I forget that God may have other laid out plans for me. I am the reflection of His image, and He has a purpose and direction for me. I am His earthly vessel and representative who should bring out His manifest purpose and achieve what He desires for His glory. I have submitted myself to be His messenger who sends out His word and speaks of awesomeness even in situations where I face calamity. Finally, the only way I see myself is through His eyes. He has brought me to this place of personal reflection as I attempt to understand what He has in store for me. It may not all be clear right now, but there is much more where this came from and what's important for now is to take my life back.

I reaffirm my thoughts and create a mantra of sorts: 'This leg will do what I want it to do. I do not do what the leg wants. It will do what I want. I want to walk, I want to stand for more than ten seconds and run, and this leg will get that job done.'

'I rigorously lament all of the many things that I don't have. But in this self-imposed and rather lively pity-party to which I've invited myself, what I forget are the resources I do have that equip me to obtain what I don't.'

Craig D. Lounsbrough

CHAPTER THIRTY-FOUR

HOW TO LOSE AN ELECTION

'Avoid aligning yourself with certain people based on their current political fortune. It will not help your career. Your whole political aspirations should be based on your inspiration of the people and the confidence and pride that they have in you.'

Robinson Zulu

The election results began to pour in at about 7pm that evening after the last ballot was cast. I can hear my mother praying in the other room as I watch my father with his ear pressed to the two-band radio and shouting out each count as it comes in. I lie almost lifeless on the bed as it slowly dawns on me that this result will not be good. Polling station after polling station, the results come in and I begin to pack my clothes in readiness for the trip back to the main district. The rest of the team is outside by the fire sitting in silence. A gentle knock on my door brings me back.

'Honourable, we need to go now.'

I roll back my eyes, grateful for the darkness as I have asked them countless times not to call me by that title, but to no avail.

'But it's 2am!' I say, wondering why the urgency in these wee hours of the morning.

'Yes, but we have to leave now before they come,' he insists.

I am tempted to ask who 'they' are but I know better. I pick up my bag and shake my mum and dad, who have fallen asleep at this point and I whisper: 'Mum, Dad, we have to leave.'

We leave quietly if not stealthily in the dead of night and the only sound that can be heard is that of the Land Rover crossing the sandy plains of Barotseland towards the pontoon on the Luanginga River. We had prearranged for the pontoon operators to be on our side of the river to cross quickly for the victory lap when we win, but alas, it is for our great escape. The solemnity at the rendezvous can be felt by all as I thank my team and watch them hold back their tears as we say our goodbyes.

'It's okay, Mummy, don't cry,' they comfort me as much as I try to comfort them.

It is 4am when I realise I haven't called my husband to tell him the election results. It is 3am in the UK, but I know he won't be sleeping, so I call.

'Hello Mummy, it's Christopher. Did you win?'

'No, I didn't, but that's okay, we ran a good race. Will you tell Daddy I called?'

'He's here; I'm in your bed, but wait, Mummy?'

'Yes?' I say.

'What happened to Nameless?'

Oh dammit! 'Christopher, I'll call you in the morning,' and I cut the line.

How could I lose an election and lose a limb in the same year? The whole thing remains a mystery to me. Actually, I lost both within a four-month period. Even die-hards like me eventually will die, I have come to believe – mortality is tested. Why must the Lord test my mortality when we both know it was certain I would join Him at the banquet, or wasn't it? Humility is tested, and that is a hard pill to swallow for anyone. I walked into that campaign blasting out my message of perceived hope, education, progress, and women's empowerment – carefully selecting key words I thought were solutions for the people I wished to serve.

I thought that the political campaign trail, with the endless talking, the endless travelling and moving about, the endless attempt to convince the mindset of the electorate about what could be a new order – sleeping in strange huts on earthen floors where you don't care about creature comforts, praying you don't wake up with aches and pains in places on your body, for you never imagined your whole body could feel as hard as an ankle joint. It is not taking for granted the headmaster's office that is offered to you amongst the entire team to get a few hours of rest before the harshness and the grind of the process all comes back in the morning where the winner takes all. I sacrificed my creature comforts and thought it was enough and what I didn't realise was that I was not in sync with what the people wanted.

I assumed I was the answer to all their problems, both known and unknown. How arrogant I was to believe that I knew the people and that I understood their way of life just because I was partly raised in my maternal grandmother's household, who was chieftainess *Mboajikana* (third ranking in the royal Lozi hierarchy) of Kalabo for over thirty years. I presumed it was my birth right to lead and guide the people the best way I knew how, but boy oh boy, was I wrong, and how totally deserving I was of that loss!

It soon became obvious that I had failed to understand my purpose. I didn't fully understand the plight of the constituents I was campaigning to and the kind of technology I needed to blast out my message of alleged hope which, in hindsight, was hopeless. Technology is easiest with today's social media platforms, but how could I have thought that radio interviews and Facebook advertising would have helped in an area with an extensive geographical diversity, with little or no radio frequency, and which is eighty-five per cent without electric or solar power? Yet, there I was carrying on as though I had it all figured out and all my bases were covered. Would campaigning in a remote area with no 3G, 4G or any other G have been useful to the constituents being campaigned to? How could I not have considered that the people needed the basic elements of life to survive: water, food, and shelter? Instead, what was my manifesto? 'Build a bridge across the Luanginga River, better education, and better health facilities.' A bridge! A bridge? Really?

That promise of a bridge cost me an election, and I lost – and indeed I deserved to lose the election on that single factor. And the timing, a mere three months prior to the date of the general election, in an area that takes a day's travel to reach 300 constituents in an area with 15,000 registered voters. So, fifty days of travel is almost two months, assuming you do not return for fuel and other reserves during that period. It was a total miscalculation on my part in many ways, and definitely another reason why I deserved to lose.

I went into Liuwa promising manna from heaven, and fortunately, the people saw right through me. They heard the false prophesy and they cast their ballots based on that. I arrogantly assumed I was the solution to their problems, yet I was the problem. I lost an election, but fortunately for me, I won something far more valuable, which I could not place a unit price on. I became a part of the people. I lived, slept, ate, danced, and cried with Liuwa. I saw Liuwa through my own eyes and not my grandmother's eyes, and I tasted the food with my buds not hers. I saw the mighty buffalo grazing as though they were cows, and from afar, they seemed harmless until you approached them to see the angry glare that instantly made you realise it was not a herd of cattle and everyone in the car would freeze, driver included. I saw the spotted hyena as we drove through Liuwa National Park and a countless number of rabbits that would run in front of the headlights, as I kept shouting at them to get out of the way. Why wouldn't they just turn left or right, and get off the track to let us pass? But the driver always had other thoughts as he increased his speed shouting, '*Ki bu sunso*', meaning an accompaniment to the main meal. But he would immediately slow down when I'd threaten to leave him in the game park in the dead of the night to give him adequate time to chase after the *bu sunso* on foot.

Finally, Liuwa was me and I was Liuwa. We were all generations of Liuwa, and I fell in love with home. I may have lost an election, but I found my soul and a greater sense of belonging. It was from the loss that I went back to say thank you to everyone who had bothered to cast a vote for this unknown person, and an even greater thank you to the ones that didn't cast their vote in my favour. They helped me to grow into the person I was becoming.

Humility is an acquired taste, bitter at first, and then one day, you stop tasting the bitterness without even realising it. Then someone would ask,

'Can't you taste it?'

'Taste what?' you ask.

'The bitterness in your mouth,' they would say.

You smile, even laugh sometimes, because it is no longer there, and what a joy it is to be on an oxcart at 0.2 miles per hour and you say to the controller, 'Slow down, we're going too fast,' which would send both of us into uncontrolled laughter.

The children ran after the ox cart shouting, 'Sweets, sweets!' and I would say to them, 'I do not have any more sweets. I, too, want sweets from someone else,' and they would shout in disbelief, 'Aaah, *Bo* Mwangala, *ma* sweetee.'

'*Anina, niti fa*,' I would shout out, trying to reassure them that indeed I didn't have any more sweets.

'*Batili Bo* Mwangala, *kimina Bo* Mwangala,' they would insist, pumping my ego to get their way.

How wonderful to be acknowledged – sweets or no sweets. I am still *Bo* Mwangala to them regardless of whether I was elected or not.

Robinson Zulu said to me upon sharing my loss and subsequent shame; 'Your whole political aspiration should be based on your inspiration of your people, and the confidence and pride that they have in you.'

He was right, and that truth remains today. I needed to align my aspirations with the people I intended to serve. A purpose that is not aligned with the aspirations of the people doesn't manifest the intent and I am eternally grateful to the people of Liuwa for the humbling learning experience, because my loss changed me. Eventually, I became part of the people. I lived there, I ate there, I slept there, hungered with them and celebrate with them. I saw at first-hand what no false prophet could see. I lost the election, but I won the battle.

My name is Mwangala Mwenda, and finally, I am a child of Liuwa.

'Nothing comes easy in life, but politics is incredibly difficult.'

Govinda[64]

CHAPTER THIRTY-FIVE
LONDON MARATHON

'One's philosophy is not best expressed in words; it is expressed in the choices one makes.'

Eleanor Roosevelt[65]

Virgin Money London Marathon, 2019.

I entered and trained for the London Marathon, and the Virgin Money Giving Fundraising account for AMREF was steadily hitting the target amount to be raised. It seemed there were people who actually believed that I could do it. The only problem was, I was not one of them; nonetheless, there was still enough zeal and stubbornness in me left; the bit that never gives up in spite of everything I had endured, and the will to reach my intended goal. The end is never out of sight, and it did not matter where the end would be as long as it was the end indeed.

The year 2016 was life-changing for me in countless ways. Being an amputee at any age is traumatising and more so at the age of forty-five, and having to learn how to walk all over again was most times harder than I could bear. Every day, I woke up hoping my leg had grown back. I had a choice to make – either I accepted my new reality or dwelt in my own pity-party. It was necessary for my self-worth to find my place in the universe and to claim a stake in my rehabilitation.

I had several reasons for wanting to take part in the London Marathon. The words 'I am still me' floated over me hauntingly, as I repeatedly tried to convince myself that although my physical appearance had changed, I had not changed, that my mindset had not changed. Once upon a time I used to be passionate about advocating for an inclusive society for women, and now here I was part of a different kettle of fish. I began to question what participatory social inclusion for persons with disabilities meant to me. I came to the realisation that trying to look to other people to include me would take a lifetime, so getting personally involved was more or less experimental with one part as a gesture of gratitude and appreciation to AMREF Health Africa, and the other to help bring the much-needed awareness to this charity that saved my life.

We could call it a moment of temporary insanity, but never had I had more conviction to be part of something than I did at that mad moment. How would a person who had just learnt to wear a prosthesis three months earlier take part in a 42km race with able-bodied people? That question became my motivation rather than my distraction. I had a goal to achieve and I would not back down from it despite the odds that were seemingly against me.

Day 1

1.32km in sixty minutes. Somebody please tell me that 42km is actually 4.2km!

I cannot handle the pressure that is being exerted on my battered body. The artificialness of my acquired limb is screaming in all its glory to remind me I am being ridiculous.

Day 135 – June 28, 2019

'Noti, wake up! We have to go,' I whispered to my sister, slightly shaking her as I didn't want to be late for the buses that would take us to the green zone.

Crowds had gathered to watch the runners in the marathon and suddenly I felt a sea of anxiety deep down and became intimidated by the fight ahead of me. I willed myself to remain focused on the race and the reason why I needed to do it. The sheer scale of the event overwhelmed me and I wanted to escape but I had someone beside me who bought into my quest and understood my passion – Nolutu, my sister.

12:20

'Noti, how much further?'

'*Bo* Mwangala, we have only done nine kilometres.'

What seems like hours later, I am begging her to stop. The stump inside the prosthesis is screaming. I hold onto every ledge I can find for support. Passers-by are stopping to check on me, and I guess they're wondering why I am doing this to myself, but I need to go on. This is a fight I can't quit now.

15:00

The St. John Ambulance is called to take us home.

'Noti, let us go home.'

'*Bo* Mwangala, if we stop now, we might as well have stopped at three kilometres.'

'Noti, *ni swale, nawa!*' I hold onto her for dear life to prevent myself from falling.

'*Bo* Mwangala, *ni mi sweli. Aluyeni.*' Reassuring me she's got me, we carry on.

Most people have finished their races in less than four hours, have got their medals and have gone home. The sun has set and everyone is now ambling away from the event route and going home. There is no point carrying on because no one will be at the finish line. What is the point really? There is no battle to fight now, no point to prove, and no awareness to be shown of the beloved charity I want to positively represent, but I can't give up now. I have come this far; we have come this far. If not for myself, at least let it be for my sister. She deserves to finish the race she trained so hard for and she was excited about being awarded the prestigious medal.

19:25

'Noti, I'm so sorry. We will not get the medals; we missed the cut-off time for medals. They have all gone.'

'*Bo* Mwangala, we will finish this race, medal or not, we will finish *our* race.'

20:30

There are strange noises, and I realise that I am the one making them. Every part of my body is hurting like crazy, and the pain is ripping through the bleeding stump in the prosthesis. Each step is an agonising new rip of searing pain, but I cannot stop now. This has become *my* race for my personal endurance and God's glorification.

21:48

'*Bo* Mwangala, we made it! We finished the London Marathon!'

I hold onto my sister tightly and weep. We made it, and there is no more we can do now. I have given it all I have, but the race official is waiting for us.

'On behalf of the Mayor of London, I am proud to present you with this medal for completing the London Marathon!'

My sister and I ran and won our race and on our terms. We did it in a proud nine hours and forty-eight minutes! We won *our* race… *and* we got *our* medals!

00:00

We eat the left-over bagels from breakfast in silence and fall asleep.

01:22

'Noti?'
'Yes, *Bo* Mwangala?'
'We got the medals?'
'Sister, we made it!'
'Noti?'
'Shyaaa?'
'Thank you.'
Finally, Nolutu is crying the tears she has held back to strengthen me.

08:00

'Adam, please come and take us home.'
Adam comes to the hotel and picks me up from my bed. I realise I have stained the hotel sheets with blood from my bleeding stump whilst I was sleeping.
'Oh no,' I worried.

'It's okay, babe, I'm sure they've seen worse. Let's get you home.'

He puts me to bed where I remain for the next six weeks with only intermittent visits to the clinic. Do I have any regrets? Absolutely and most definitely not. Would I do it again? Absolutely and most definitely not. The race was significant to me, and it represented a big part of what I wanted for myself and my future. I carved a place for myself in my universe with blood and tears. I won my race. We won our race!

'Mummy, we are so proud of you,' they say in unison with beaming faces.

'Mummy, can I wear your medal?' a beaming AJ asks.

My kids can finally learn that whatever life throws at them, they should never give up because they might even get a medal at the end.

'Lord, we did it!' and I imagine a beaming Lord, smiling down at me with a twinkle in His eye, as He says to me, 'I KNOW.'

'The most glorious moment you will ever experience in your life is when you look back and see how God was protecting you all this time.'

Shannon L. Alder

CHAPTER THIRTY-SIX

BLESSED ASSURANCE

'The Lord is good to all, and his mercy is over all that he has made.'

Psalm 145:9[66]

Am I completely healed, or blissfully happy, or has fear finally left me? Not at all. It is rather that I am stepping out of my self-imposed cage as I come to terms with my new self. Not being the person I used to be is probably not such a bad thing for I have been given the Grace to relive and reboot my life. I have forgiven and I am forgiven. Enough of the pity-partying; it has exhausted me. The dancing and singing to the same old songs, the same drinks all the time, which no longer have priority in my new-found space of personal comfort and peace. Someone clever once said: 'You only have to forgive once. To resent, you have to do it all, every day.'[67] That is too much work. It is time to turn off the music.

My journey of self-discovery has made me realise how easy it is to die without ever knowing how close you came to living. The new and old me can live in harmony without battling for precedence. Denial, depression and forgiveness have flip sides that can represent acceptance, peace, and resilience.

As I look to the future aspirations in this new phase of my life, the political arena continues to beckon, new adventures await my exploration, my story is rebirthed as I continue to stand and sing a new song.

1. *Blessed assurance, Jesus is mine!*
   Oh, what a foretaste of glory divine!
   Heir of salvation, purchase of God,
   Born of His Spirit, washed in His blood.

   Refrain:
   This is my story, this is my song,
   Praising my Saviour all the day long;
   This is my story, this is my song,
   Praising my Saviour all the day long.

2. *Perfect submission, perfect delight,*
   Visions of rapture now burst on my sight;
   Angels, descending, bring from above
   Echoes of mercy, whispers of love.

3. Perfect submission, all is at rest,
   I in my Saviour am happy and blest,
   Watching and waiting, looking above,
   Filled with His goodness, lost in His love.

Frances J. Crosby, 1873[68]

'I will not let you go, unless you bless me.'

Genesis 32:26

ACKNOWLEDGEMENTS

To my husband, Adam Lethbridge, your unconditional love and support held all my pieces together.

To my children, Kelvin, Nina, Christopher, and Adam-James (AJ), I continue to live for you.

To Ian Musweu, for everything.

To Steve Mulembeta, for never giving up on me.

To Patrick Nswana, for helping me redefine forgiveness.

To my half-life, Clara, for the comfortable silence we have always shared.

To Laura Celli and Alberto Scocco, first they were two, and then one, but you remained steadfast.

To my dear friends: Usha, Shenda, Inonge, Mukwandi, Namwinga and Womba, I can never thank you enough.

To Brenda, short, yet fulfilled life. I am still in awe of you, my friend.

To the unknown taxi driver, for your selfless act of compassion, thank you.

To my friend and mentor, John Sangwa SC, for being *my person*.

To *Mukwae* Inonge Mutukwa Wina, for your continued guidance.

To my 'advisor', Robinson Zulu, your counsel has helped to change my perception of politics and life.

To Trauma 3 Unit at the John Radcliffe Hospital in the UK, the Italian Orthopaedic Hospital in Zambia, the Physiotherapy Clinic at the Royal Berkshire in the UK, you have no idea how you all positively impacted my life.

To Class of '87, the anonymous blood donors, and to everyone that extended their support, I say 'thank you' to you all.

To my parents. Your ongoing faith, prayers and support, yesterday and always, have made me believe that we serve a living God. I love you.

To all my *Still Standing* family who have graciously given me their permission to share our conversations in this memoir, thank you.

BIBLIOGRAPHY

1. Goodreads.com. (2020). *A quote from Wuthering Heights*. [online] Available at: https://www.goodreads.com/quotes/107921-heaven-did-not-seem-to-be-my-home-and-i [Accessed 12 Dec. 2020]
2. BrainyQuote. (2020). *Friedrich Nietzsche Quotes*. [online] Available at: https://www.brainyquote.com/quotes/friedrich_nietzsche_105845 [Accessed 12 Dec. 2020].
3. https://www.lowerzambezi.com/
4. McDreamy https://en.wikipedia.org/wiki/Derek_Shepherd
5. African Medical Research Foundation (AMREF) https://www.who.int/workforcealliance/members_partners/member_list/amref/en/
6. Goodreads.com. (2020). *A quote from Unapologetically You*. [online] Available at: https://www.goodreads.com/quotes/319550-it-s-funny-how-in-this-journey-of-life-even-though [Accessed 12 Dec. 2020].
7. Abhijit Naskar, Build Bridges not Walls: In the name of Americana https://www.goodreads.com/work/quotes/66941816-build-bridges-not-walls-in-the-name-of-americana
8. Contributor, N. and Contributor, N. (2019). The underlying principles and procedure for bed bathing patients | Nursing Times. [online] Nursing Times. Available at: https://www.nursingtimes.net/roles/hospital-nurses/the-underlying-principles-and-procedure-for-bed-bathing-patients-25-04-2019/
9. Goodreads.com. (2020). A quote from Landscape of the Body. [online] Available at: https://www.goodreads.com/quotes/1012503-it-s-amazing-how-a-little-tomorrow-can-make-up-for [Accessed 12 Dec. 2020]. Landscape of the Body

10 G. D. Morgan https://theunboundedspirit.com/250-motivational-quotes-sayings-on-will-power-success-determination-and-more/
11 Brainy Quote (2020) Mark Twain Quotes [online] Available at: https://www.brainyquote.com/quotes/mark_twain_109919 [Accessed 12 Dec. 2020].
12 Corrie Ten Boom https://www.brainyquote.com/quotes/corrie_ten_boom_135203
13 Piper, J. (2018). God's Sovereign Plans Behind Your Most Unproductive Days [online] Desiring God. Available at: https://www.desiringgod.org/interviews/gods-sovereign-plans-behind-your-most-unproductive-days [Accessed 13 Sep. 2020]
14 Viktor E. Frankl https://www.goodreads.com/quotes/51356-everything-can-be-taken-from-a-man-but-one-thing
15 Goodreads.com. (2020). A quote by Brené Brown [online] Available at: https://www.goodreads.com/quotes/544060-if-you-trade-your-authenticity-for-safety-you-may-experience [Accessed 13 Dec. 2020].
16 George Sand https://www.brainyquote.com/quotes/george_sand_154922
17 Henry Ford https://www.goodreads.com/quotes/24623-obstacles-are-those-frightful-things-you-see-when-you-take
18 Goodreads.com. (2021). A quote from The Proud Highway. [online] Available at: https://www.goodreads.com/quotes/47188-life-should-not-be-a-journey-to-the-grave-with [Accessed 13 Apr. 2021]
19 'River Wild' by Hillsong https://hillsong.com/collected/ru/blog/2015/11/transfiguration-song-story/#.Xz-vQugzbIU
20 Phoebe Stone https://www.goodreads.com/quotes/875111-i-am-told-many-children-block-out-the-memory-of
21 Goodreads.com. (2021). A quote from The Proud Highway. [online] Available at: https://www.goodreads.com/quotes/47188-life-should-not-be-a-journey-to-the-grave-with [Accessed 13 Apr. 2021].
22 J.R. Ward https://www.goodreads.com/quotes/529618-then-again-he-supposed-the-healing-process-in-contrast-to
23 Goodreads.com. (2021). A quote from The Proud Highway. [online] Available at: https://www.goodreads.com/quotes/47188-life-should-not-be-a-journey-to-the-grave-with [Accessed 13 Apr. 2021]
24 Goodreads.com. (2020). A quote from MI VIDA. [online] Available at: https://www.goodreads.com/quotes/416345-tears-shed-for-another-person-are-not-a-sign-of [Accessed 8 Dec. 2020]. Mi Vida: A Story of Faith, Hope and Love
25 Pedia, Q. (2019). When you reach the end of your rope, tie a knot in it and hang on – Franklin D. Roosevelt – Quotes Pedia – Available at: https://www.quotespedia.org/authors/f/franklin-d-roosevelt/when-you-reach-the-end-of-your-rope-tie-a-knot-in-it-and-hang-on-franklin-d-roosevelt/ [Accessed 8 Dec. 2020]

26 Danielle Bernock, 'Emerging With Wings: A True Story of Lies, Pain, and the Love that Heals' https://www.goodreads.com/en/book/show/23465091-emerging-with-wings

27 Goodreads.com. (2020). A quote by G.K. Chesterton. [online] Available at: https://www.goodreads.com/quotes/341193-fairy-tales-do-not-tell-children-the-dragons-exist-children [Accessed 8 Dec. 2020].

28 Gay Byrne https://www.independent.co.uk/news/world/europe/stephen-fry-blasphemy-god-ireland-police-investigation-quotes-in-full-a7722256.html

29 Collateral Beauty https://en.wikipedia.org/wiki/Collateral_Beauty

30 Goodreads.com (2020) A quote by G.K. Chesterton [online] Available at: https://www.goodreads.com/quotes/341193-fairy-tales-do-not-tell-children-the-dragons-exist-children [Accessed 8 Dec. 2020]

31 Goodreads.com. (2020). A quote by G.K. Chesterton. [online] Available at: https://www.goodreads.com/quotes/341193-fairy-tales-do-not-tell-children-the-dragons-exist-children [Accessed 8 Dec. 2020]

32 Chuang-Tzu and Wu, K. (2020) The Butterfly as Companion. [online] Goodreads.com. Available at: https://www.goodreads.com/book/show/848403.The_Butterfly_as_Companion [Accessed 20 Oct. 2020]

33 Fred Rogers https://www.goodreads.com/quotes/157666-anything-that-s-human-is-mentionable-and-anything-that-is-mentionable

34 A quote from *The River of Winged Dreams* [online] Available at: https://www.goodreads.com/quotes/498905-un-winged-and-naked-sorrow-surrenders-its-crown-to-a-throne [Accessed 20 Oct 2020]

35 Albert Camus https://www.goodreads.com/quotes/2313-in-the-depth-of-winter-i-finally-learned-that-within

36 Our Everyday Life (2020) How to Deal With Overbearing Sisters [online] Available at: https://oureverydaylife.com/deal-overbearing-sisters-12167658.html [Accessed 18 Oct 2020]

37 En.wikivoyage.org (2020) Manchester – Travel guide at Wikivoyage. [online] Available at: https://en.wikivoyage.org/wiki/Manchester [Accessed 19 Oct 2020]

38 Christine Mason Miller https://www.goodreads.com/quotes/1119001-at-any-given-moment-you-have-the-power-to-say

39 Akshay Dubey https://www.goodreads.com/quotes/1274987-healing-doesn-t-mean-the-damage-never-existed-it-means-the

40 International University of Monaco. (2013). The real challenge facing business schools and MBA programs – International University of Monaco. [online] Available at: https://www.monaco.edu/news-business-school/making-the-magic-triangle-work-the-real-challenge-facing-business-schools-and-mba-programs/ [Accessed 21 Oct 2020]

41 En.wikipedia.org. (2020). List of Grey's Anatomy episodes. [online] Available at: https://en.wikipedia.org/wiki/List_of_Grey%27s_Anatomy_episodes#:~:text=The%20series%20was%20created%20to%20be%20racially%20diverse%2C,broadcast%20on%20Thursday%20nights%20since%20Grey%27s%20third%20season. [Accessed 21 Oct. 2020]
42 Mary Anne Radmacher https://www.goodreads.com/author/quotes/149829.Mary_Anne_Radmacher
43 Plato https://www.azquotes.com/quote/851808
44 Idle Hearts (2020) Part of the problem with the word 'disabilities' is that it immediately. [online] Available at: https://www.idlehearts.com/797220/part-of-the-problem-with-the-word-disabilities-is-that-it-immediately [Accessed 10 Dec. 2020]. The World According to Mister Rogers: Important Things to Remember
45 Goodreads.com. (2020). Getting Better Quotes (21 quotes). [online] Available at: https://www.goodreads.com/quotes/tag/getting-better [Accessed 4 Dec. 2020]
46 Behaviour and Whaley, J. (2020). Highly Illogical Behaviour. [online] Goodreads.com. Available at: https://www.goodreads.com/book/show/26109391-highly-illogical-behavior#:~:text=Highly%20Illogical%20Behavior%20is%20a%20sweet%20coming%20of,touch%20of%20empathy%20that%20readers%20will%20also%20experience. [Accessed 4 Dec. 2020]
47 Fdrlibrary.org. (2020). Eleanor Roosevelt – FDR Presidential Library & Museum. [online] Available at: https://www.fdrlibrary.org/eleanor-roosevelt [Accessed 8 Dec. 2020] You Learn by Living: Eleven Keys for a More Fulfilling Life
48 Goodreads.com. (2020). A quote by Nikki Rowe. [online] Available at: https://www.goodreads.com/quotes/8084466-give-yourself-permission-to-let-it-hurt-but-also-allow [Accessed 8 Dec. 2020]
49 Jeffrey Pfeffer's https://www.goodreads.com/book/show/24331490-leadership-bs
50 Maya Angelou https://www.nytimes.com/1993/01/21/us/the-inauguration-maya-angelou-on-the-pulse-of-morning.html
51 Kiana Lede https://www.youtube.com/watch?v=VAe5IdtpsGs
52 CeCe Winans https://www.youtube.com/watch?v=sXyIojnR6rw
53 Katelyn Tarver https://www.youtube.com/watch?v=BF-nZziUCCY
54 Quotefancy.com. (2020). Elena Ferrante Quote: 'I'm lying, yes, but why do you force me to give a linear explanation; linear explanations are almost always lies.' [online] Available at: https://quotefancy.com/quote/2263967/Elena-Ferrante-I-m-lying-yes-but-why-do-you-force-me-to-give-a-linear-explanation-linear [Accessed 8 Dec. 2020]
55 Margaret Thatcher https://www.brainyquote.com/quotes/margaret_thatcher_127095

BIBLIOGRAPHY

56 Tameela Manns https://www.youtube.com/watch?v=wU3qgPn3bGA

57 Juanita Bynum https://zionlyrics.com/juanita-bynum-i-dont-mind-waiting-praise-your-way-out-inspirational-lyrics

58 Andrea Gibson, The Madness Vase https://www.amazon.com/Madness-Vase-Andrea-Gibson/dp/193590437X

59 Bible.com. (2020). Matthew 11:28-30 Come to me, all who labour and are heavy laden, and I will give you rest. Take my yoke upon you, and learn from me, for I am gentle and lowly in heart, and you will find rest for your souls. For my yok | English Standard Version 2016 (ESV) | Download The Bible App Now. [online] Available at: https://www.bible.com/bible/59/MAT.11.28-30.ESV [Accessed 18 Oct. 2020]

60 User, S. (2020). History of Lent. [online] Catholiceducation.org. Available at: https://www.catholiceducation.org/en/culture/catholic-contributions/history-of-lent.html [Accessed 28 Sep. 2020]

61 Myles Monroe 'Fasting 101 – How to Fast Efficiently'

62 https://www.goodreads.com/work/quotes/13462590-one-thousand-gifts

63 Goodreads.com. (2020). A quote from Daily Drive 365. [online] Available at: https://www.goodreads.com/quotes/7178676-stop-the-pity-party-your-sorrow-is-full-and-complete [Accessed 7 Dec. 2020]

64 Govinda https://www.brainyquote.com/quotes/govinda_982359

65 Eleanor Roosevelt https://www.goodreads.com/quotes/202842-one-s-philosophy-is-not-best-expressed-in-words-it-is

66 Bible Gateway. (2020). Bible Gateway passage: Psalm 145:4, Psalm 145 – English Standard Version. [online] Available at: https://www.biblegateway.com/passage/?search=Psalm+145%3A4%2CPsalm+145&version=ESV [Accessed 6 Dec. 2020]

67 ML Stedman, The Light Between Oceans https://www.goodreads.com/quotes/621136-you-only-have-to-forgive-once-to-resent-you-have

68 Frances J. Crosby, 1873 https://library.timelesstruths.org/music/Blessed_Assurance/

This book is printed on paper from sustainable sources managed under the Forest Stewardship Council (FSC) scheme.

It has been printed in the UK to reduce transportation miles and their impact upon the environment.

For every new title that Matador publishes, we plant a tree to offset CO_2, partnering with the More Trees scheme.

For more about how Matador offsets its environmental impact, see www.troubador.co.uk/about/